UNLOCKING GENIUS

Life-Changing Lessons from the Minds of History's Greatest Thinkers

FELIX GRAYSON

MINDSPARK
PUBLISHING

To the seekers, the dreamers, and the brave souls who dare to embrace their potential — this book is for you. Your courage to grow, to question, and to create inspires the world.

"Everyone has a genius. It is just to bring it out. To nurture it. To feed it."

— *Elizabeth Gilbert*

ABOUT STONED PHILOSOPHER

Welcome to the *Stoned Philosopher* series—where timeless wisdom meets the modern world.

Each book distills powerful lessons from history's greatest minds, leaders, and thinkers—transforming their ideas into practical insights for today's challenges.

From mastering habits, calm, and resilience to understanding success, leadership, and meaning, this collection invites you to think deeper, live wiser, and see life from new perspectives.

Whether you're exploring *Modern Zen*, uncovering *The Wisdom of Warriors*, or seeking clarity through *The Art of Perspective*, every title offers a journey toward self-mastery and understanding.

Discover the full *Stoned Philosopher* collection and more at **FelixGrayson.com**, home of **MindSpark Publishing**—where knowledge, philosophy, and storytelling come together to spark lifelong curiosity.

FelixGrayson.com 🔍

Wisdom isn't something we find—it's something we grow into.

Let the journey begin.

CONTENTS

INTRODUCTION: THE GENIUS WITHIN **10**

CHAPTER 1: THE NATURE OF GENIUS –
UNDERSTANDING EXTRAORDINARY MINDS 17

Defining Genius Across Cultures 18

The Science Behind Genius 23

Nature Versus Nurture 29

Awakening Your Inner Genius 36

CHAPTER 2: VISION AND IMAGINATION – THE
SEEDS OF INNOVATION **43**

The Role of Imagination in Historical Breakthroughs
.... 44

Barriers to Creativity 50

Cultivating a Visionary Mindset 58

The Modern Application of Vision 65

CHAPTER 3: MASTERY THROUGH FOCUS – THE POWER OF DEEP WORK 73

The Art of Sustained Focus 74

The Challenges of Modern Distractions 79

Building the Discipline of Deep Work 86

The Rewards of Mastery 93

CHAPTER 4: THE COURAGE TO FAIL – LESSONS FROM BOLD INNOVATORS 101

The Role of Failure in Genius 102

Overcoming Fear of Failure 107

Turning Setbacks into Stepping Stones 115

Embracing Failure as a Process 122

CHAPTER 5: THE POWER OF COLLABORATION – GENIUS IN TEAMWORK 130

Historical Collaborations That Changed the World
.... 131

Balancing Independence and Teamwork 137

Building Effective Partnerships 145

The Future of Collaboration 152

CHAPTER 6: THE ROLE OF CURIOSITY – A LIFELONG QUEST FOR KNOWLEDGE 161

Curiosity as the Engine of Discovery 162

Rekindling Childlike Wonder 168

Practical Tools for Lifelong Learning 175

Resisting Intellectual Complacency 182

CHAPTER 7: GENIUS AND EMOTIONAL INTELLIGENCE – BALANCING HEART AND MIND 189

The Interplay Between Emotion and Intellect 190

Understanding and Regulating Emotions 196

Building Empathy and Social Awareness 203

Emotional Resilience and Genius 210

CHAPTER 8: UNLOCKING YOUR GENIUS – A BLUEPRINT FOR GREATNESS 218

Synthesizing the Lessons 219

Developing a Personalized Framework 225

Cultivating a Growth-Oriented Lifestyle 232

The Call to Greatness 238

CONCLUSION: A JOURNEY TOWARD GENIUS 245

INTRODUCTION: THE GENIUS WITHIN

What makes a genius? Is it an extraordinary intellect, an unmatched talent, or a rare spark of creativity that sets certain individuals apart? For centuries, society has revered genius as something almost mythical—a gift bestowed upon a select few, inaccessible to the rest of us. But what if that narrative is incomplete? What if genius is not a fixed trait but a dynamic process, one that is available to anyone willing to pursue it with curiosity, focus, and resilience?

This book begins with a simple yet transformative premise: Genius is within reach. It is not the exclusive domain of prodigies or pioneers; it is a quality that lies dormant in each of us, waiting to be awakened. Unlocking your genius does not require perfect circumstances or superhuman abilities. It requires intention, effort, and a willingness to see challenges as opportunities.

A World Shaped by Genius

From the moment humankind first gazed at the stars and wondered about the cosmos, genius has driven us forward. It is the force behind history's greatest discoveries, from Galileo's celestial revelations to Marie Curie's ground-breaking work on radiation. It is the thread that connects the art of Leonardo da Vinci to the activism of Martin Luther King Jr., the poetry of Maya Angelou to the technological innovations of Steve Jobs.

But genius is not confined to the pages of history books. It is the entrepreneur who dares to challenge convention, the teacher who ignites a love of learning, the artist who paints emotions into life, and the parent who nurtures curiosity and resilience in their child. Genius is all around us—woven into the fabric of human experience, accessible to anyone who dares to seek it.

The Purpose of This Book

This book is a blueprint for unlocking your potential. It is not a manual for perfection, nor is it a promise of instant transformation. Instead, it is a guide to understanding the principles that underpin genius and how to apply them in your own life. These principles—curiosity, focus, emotional intelligence, collaboration, resilience, and vision—are the building blocks of greatness. They are not exclusive traits but skills that can be cultivated through deliberate practice and intention.

Each chapter of this book explores one of these principles in depth, weaving together historical examples, psychological insights, and practical applications. You will learn how Galileo's insatiable curiosity redefined our understanding of the universe and how Michelangelo's focus brought the Sistine Chapel to life. You will discover how emotional intelligence fueled Gandhi's leadership, how collaboration propelled The Beatles to global stardom, and how resilience carried J.K. Rowling from rejection to worldwide acclaim.

But this is not just a book about others' journeys—it is a book about yours. At every step, you will be invited to reflect, challenge yourself, and apply the lessons to your own life. The goal is not to emulate history's greatest minds but to unlock the unique genius that resides within you.

Why Genius Matters Now More Than Ever

We live in a world that is both profoundly in-terconnected and deeply complex. The chal-lenges we face—climate change, technological disruption, social inequality—demand inno-vative solutions and bold leadership. At the same time, the rapid pace of change can leave us feeling overwhelmed and disconnected from our own potential.

In this context, unlocking your genius is not just a personal pursuit; it is a contribution to the greater good. Genius is not about individ-ual accolades but about making a meaningful impact—whether that means solving a global problem, creating art that inspires, or simply living a life of authenticity and purpose.

As you embark on this journey, consider the ripple effect of your actions. By cultivating your own potential, you not only transform your life but also inspire and uplift those around you. Your genius has the power to shape not only your future but the future of the world.

What Awaits You in These Pages

This book is structured as a journey, beginning with an exploration of the nature of genius and its many dimensions. Each chapter builds on the last, offering insights and tools to help you cultivate the principles of greatness:

- **Curiosity** ignites the spark of discovery, pushing you to explore, question, and imagine what is possible.

- **Focus** transforms that spark into mastery, allowing you to channel your efforts with precision and discipline.

- **Emotional Intelligence** bridges the gap between heart and mind, enhancing your ability to connect, lead, and navigate challenges.

- **Collaboration** amplifies your strengths through teamwork and shared purpose, proving that genius is rarely a solitary endeavor.

- **Resilience** provides the foundation for enduring setbacks and continuing forward with courage and determination.

- **Vision** guides you toward a life of purpose and impact, aligning your actions with your highest aspirations.

The final chapter synthesizes these lessons, offering a blueprint for unlocking your genius and creating a life of growth, contribution, and fulfillment.

An Invitation to Begin

As you hold this book in your hands, you have already taken the first step. You have expressed curiosity—the willingness to explore and learn. That curiosity is the seed of genius, and with each page, you will nurture it into something extraordinary.

But this journey is not about passively absorbing information. It is about action, reflection, and transformation. It is about asking yourself, "What is my potential? How can I contribute? What legacy do I want to leave?" It is about embracing the challenges that lie ahead and trusting in your ability to grow through them.

The journey of genius is not a straight path, nor is it a predictable one. It is filled with twists, turns, and moments of doubt. But it is also a journey of discovery, joy, and profound fulfill-ment. Along the way, you will uncover not only what you are capable of but also who you are meant to become.

Let this book be your guide, your companion, and your call to greatness. The spark of genius is already within you. All that remains is to unlock it.

CHAPTER 1: THE NATURE OF GENIUS – UNDERSTANDING EXTRAORDINARY MINDS

Defining Genius Across Cultures

What is genius? It's a question as old as humanity's fascination with greatness itself, and yet the answer is as elusive as it is profound. The concept of genius has evolved dramatically over time, shaped by cultural values, philosophical debates, and historical events. To define it is not merely to capture a trait or a quality, but to engage with the aspirations, limitations, and triumphs of the human spirit across centuries.

The Western Lens: Genius as Divine Favor

In Western history, the idea of genius often carried a mystical quality, originating in ancient Rome. The Latin word *genius* referred to a guiding spirit or deity that protected a person or place, embodying creative energy and inspiration. This early notion suggested that genius was not an inherent trait but a force bestowed upon individuals by external, often divine, sources. Philosophers and artists of the time sought to align themselves with this transcendent force, believing it to be the key to extraordinary achievements.

The Renaissance marked a significant shift in this perception. Figures like Leonardo da Vinci and Michelangelo were celebrated not merely as vessels of divine inspiration but as individuals whose unique capabilities elevated them above their peers. Genius became synonymous with human potential, a blend of intellectual prowess and creative brilliance. The Enlightenment further reinforced this view, emphasizing reason and individualism. Thinkers like Immanuel Kant argued that genius was the ability to create something original and universally admired, a hallmark of human greatness.

The Eastern Perspective: Genius as Harmony with the Universe

In contrast, Eastern philosophies often viewed genius not as a rare and individualistic trait but as an extension of one's alignment with the natural world. Confucian thought, for example, emphasized the cultivation of virtue and wisdom through discipline and harmony. Genius, in this context, was not an isolated spark but the culmination of a life lived in accordance with universal principles.

Similarly, Taoist philosophy, with its emphasis on the Tao or "the Way," regarded exceptional abilities as a reflection of one's attunement to the flow of life. Laozi's teachings suggest that the greatest thinkers and creators achieve their feats not through force or struggle but by yielding to the natural rhythms of existence. This perspective highlights the interconnectedness of genius and humility, encouraging individuals to see themselves as part of a greater whole.

The Crossroads of East and West: A Modern Synthesis

In today's globalized world, these differing views of genius have begun to converge, offering a more nuanced understanding. Western notions of individual brilliance are increasingly tempered by Eastern ideas of balance and interconnectedness. Modern psychology, for instance, recognizes the role of both innate traits and environmental influences in fostering genius. Creativity is no longer seen as the solitary act of a "lone genius" but as a collaborative and dynamic process influenced by culture, relationships, and context.

Consider the example of Albert Einstein, often hailed as the epitome of Western scientific genius. While his groundbreaking theories reshaped our understanding of the universe, Einstein himself acknowledged the collaborative nature of his work. He famously stated, "I stand on the shoulders of giants," a nod to the interconnected web of discoveries that paved the way for his own insights. This humility resonates with Eastern philosophies, illustrating that even the most extraordinary minds do not exist in isolation.

The Evolution of Genius Over Time

The journey of defining genius is also a story of societal change. In the 19th century, Romanticism celebrated the image of the tortured genius, a solitary figure whose brilliance came at the cost of emotional turmoil. Artists like Vincent van Gogh epitomized this archetype, their work driven by intense passion and struggle. However, this romanticized view has given way to a more balanced understanding in contemporary times.

Today, the focus has shifted to the intersection

of creativity, resilience, and collaboration. Genius is no longer confined to the realms of art or science; it manifests in diverse fields, from entrepreneurship to social activism. Figures like Malala Yousafzai, who combines courage, vision, and intellect, exemplify how genius can transcend traditional boundaries, inspiring collective action and societal change.

The Call to Recognize and Redefine Genius

As we reflect on the cultural and historical definitions of genius, a compelling question arises: What does genius mean for us today? Perhaps it is not a title bestowed upon the rare few but a quality that lies dormant within each of us, waiting to be awakened. By learning from the wisdom of history's greatest thinkers, we can begin to see genius not as an unattainable ideal but as a deeply human capacity for growth, creativity, and transformation.

The journey to unlock your inner genius begins here—not by comparing yourself to the towering figures of the past, but by understanding the principles and practices that allowed them to rise above their circumstances. Whether through the harmony of Eastern philosophies or the ambition of Western ideals, the essence of genius lies in our ability to learn, adapt, and create. The chapters ahead will explore how this timeless potential can be harnessed to navigate the complexities of modern life.

The Science Behind Genius

Genius has long been the subject of fascination, but it is only in the past century that science has begun to unravel its mysteries. What distinguishes a genius from the rest of us? Is it an exceptional IQ, unparalleled creativity, or something more nuanced—a combination of traits that manifest uniquely in extraordinary individuals? Through the lenses of psychology and neuroscience, we can begin to uncover the mechanisms that drive genius, offering insights not only into the minds of history's great thinkers but also into our own untapped potential.

The Role of Intelligence: Beyond the IQ Test

For much of the 20th century, genius was closely associated with high intelligence as measured by IQ tests. These tests, designed to quantify intellectual capabilities, provided a straight-forward, if limited, metric for identifying exceptional minds. Figures like Albert Einstein and Marie Curie, often associated with genius, would undoubtedly score at the upper end of such scales. However, IQ alone does not account for the breadth of their contributions.

Modern psychologists argue that intelligence is multifaceted, encompassing logical reasoning, emotional awareness, and creative problem-solving. Howard Gardner's theory of multiple intelligences expands this view, proposing that linguistic, spatial, interpersonal, and even kinesthetic abilities are integral to human genius. By this measure, a poet like Maya Angelou, a choreographer like Martha Graham, or a diplomat like Nelson Mandela could each be considered geniuses in their respective fields. Intelligence, then, is not a singular attribute but a constellation of skills that interact to produce brilliance.

Creativity: The Heart of Genius

If intelligence provides the foundation, creativity is the spark that ignites genius. Neuroscience has revealed fascinating insights into the creative mind, showing how different regions of the brain work together to generate novel ideas. The prefrontal cortex, responsible for complex thought and decision-making, plays a key role in this process, as does the default mode network—a collection of brain regions active during moments of rest and introspection.

Interestingly, creativity often flourishes in periods of apparent idleness. Consider the famous story of Isaac Newton, who conceptualized the laws of gravity while observing a falling apple. Or think of Archimedes, who exclaimed "Eureka!" after solving a complex problem during a bath. These anecdotes highlight a critical aspect of creative genius: the ability to make connections between seemingly unrelated ideas. Psychologists call this "divergent thinking," and it is a hallmark of creative problem-solving.

Recent studies suggest that fostering creativity is not merely the domain of the naturally gifted but a skill that can be cultivated. Practices like brainstorming, mind mapping, and even daydreaming have been shown to enhance creative thinking. This democratization of creativity challenges the notion that genius is the exclusive realm of a select few, offering hope that anyone can develop their own unique brand of brilliance.

The Problem-Solving Brain: Insights from Neuroscience

One of the most striking features of genius is the ability to solve problems that seem insurmountable to others. Neuroscientists studying this phenomenon have identified a crucial factor: the capacity for sustained focus. Through techniques like functional MRI, researchers have observed how the brains of exceptional problem-solvers operate differently from the average person's. When confronted with a challenge, geniuses exhibit heightened activity in areas associated with working memory and cognitive control, allowing them to hold complex information in mind while exploring potential solutions.

However, problem-solving genius is not merely a matter of brainpower—it also requires resilience and adaptability. Thomas Edison, whose relentless experimentation led to the invention of the light bulb, famously remarked, "I have not failed. I've just found 10,000 ways that won't work." This willingness to persist in the face of setbacks reflects a mindset that prioritizes learning over immediate success, a trait supported by research on growth mindset. Coined by psychologist Carol Dweck, the concept of growth mindset emphasizes the importance of viewing challenges as opportunities for growth rather than as barriers to achievement.

The Genius Brain: Myth or Reality?

Is the brain of a genius fundamentally different from that of an average person? While the basic structure of the brain is remarkably consistent across individuals, studies have identified subtle differences in the brains of highly gifted individuals. For example, Einstein's brain, studied after his death, showed an unusually high density of neurons in regions associated with mathematical reasoning and spatial visualization. Similarly, musicians and artists often exhibit enhanced connectivity between the left and right hemispheres of the brain, enabling greater integration of analytical and creative processes.

Yet, these findings should not be interpreted as a blueprint for genius. Rather, they underscore the brain's incredible plasticity—its ability to adapt and rewire itself in response to learning and experience. The concept of neuroplasticity suggests that genius is not a fixed state but a dynamic process, shaped by effort, practice, and environment. This offers an empowering message: while we may not all possess Einstein's unique neural architecture, we are capable of extraordinary growth and achievement through deliberate effort.

Bringing Science into Daily Life

Understanding the science of genius has profound implications for our own lives. By cultivating the traits associated with exceptional minds—intelligence, creativity, focus, and resilience—we can unlock new levels of personal and professional achievement. Practical strategies such as engaging in lifelong learning, practicing mindfulness, and embracing challenges can help us harness the principles of genius in our daily lives.

Moreover, the scientific study of genius reminds us of the potential for greatness that lies within each of us. Genius is not a static label reserved for the chosen few; it is a dynamic interplay of traits and habits that anyone can develop. As we delve deeper into the nature of genius, we will uncover not only what makes extraordinary minds exceptional but also how we can apply these lessons to our own journeys of growth and discovery.

Nature Versus Nurture

Is genius born or made? This question has sparked centuries of debate among philosophers, scientists, and psychologists. On one side lies the argument that genius is an innate quality—a rare genetic gift bestowed upon a fortunate few. On the other is the belief that genius arises from effort, discipline, and the right environment. The truth, as history and science reveal, is far more complex. Genius emerges not from a singular source but from a dynamic interplay between nature and nurture, each contributing to the alchemy of greatness.

The Case for Nature: Genius as a Gift

Throughout history, countless examples have been cited to support the idea that genius is an inborn trait. Wolfgang Amadeus Mozart, for instance, is often considered a prodigy whose genius manifested at an astonishingly young age. By the age of five, he was composing music that astonished even seasoned musicians. Such precocious talent seems to suggest that genius is encoded in our DNA, a gift that reveals itself in early childhood and sets certain individuals apart from the rest.

Modern genetics lends some credence to this view. Research has identified specific genes associated with traits like intelligence, creativity, and memory. These genetic markers, combined with innate brain structures, may predispose individuals to exceptional abilities. For instance, studies on the brains of highly intelligent individuals reveal unique patterns of neural connectivity and enhanced activity in certain regions, suggesting that biology does play a role in shaping genius.

However, even Mozart's story complicates the narrative of innate genius. His early exposure to music, guided by his father—a skilled composer and teacher—provided an environment that nurtured his natural abilities. This raises an essential question: Is genius purely a genetic lottery, or does it require fertile ground in which to grow?

The Argument for Nurture: Genius as Effort and Opportunity

In contrast to the notion of inborn genius, many argue that greatness arises from persistence, education, and a supportive environment. Thomas Edison, one of history's most prolific inventors, famously stated, "Genius is one percent inspiration and ninety-nine percent perspiration." Edison's life embodies this principle. Unlike Mozart, he showed no early signs of extraordinary talent. Instead, his genius emerged through relentless experimentation and a tireless work ethic, culminating in over a thousand patents and inventions that transformed the modern world.

Psychologist Anders Ericsson's research on deliberate practice offers a compelling framework for understanding the role of effort in genius.

His "10,000-hour rule," popularized by Malcolm Gladwell, suggests that expertise—and perhaps even genius—can be achieved through consistent, focused practice over time. This perspective highlights the transformative power of dedication, implying that extraordinary achievements are accessible to anyone willing to invest the necessary effort.

Historical figures like Benjamin Franklin further illustrate the impact of nurture. Born into modest circumstances, Franklin received little formal education. Yet, through self-directed learning and an insatiable curiosity, he became a polymath whose contributions spanned science, politics, and literature. Franklin's life underscores the idea that genius is not solely a matter of innate talent but a product of self-discipline and resourcefulness.

The Interplay Between Nature and Nurture

As compelling as the arguments for nature and nurture are, the most accurate explanation lies in their interplay. Genius is neither purely inborn nor entirely cultivated—it is a synergy of inherent potential and external influences.

Albert Einstein provides a striking example of this dynamic. While his natural aptitude for abstract thought and mathematical reasoning set him apart, his achievements in physics were equally shaped by the intellectual climate of his time and the mentorship he received.

The role of environment in nurturing genius cannot be overstated. In her book *The Genius in All of Us,* author David Shenk emphasizes that talent thrives in environments that provide stimulation, support, and challenges. Historical "genius clusters" like Renaissance Florence or 20th-century Silicon Valley further illustrate this point. These hubs of creativity and innovation fostered extraordinary achievements by providing fertile ground for collaboration, competition, and inspiration.

Moreover, adversity often plays a paradoxical role in shaping genius. Figures like Frida Kahlo, who overcame physical and emotional hardships, or Nelson Mandela, who endured decades of imprisonment, demonstrate how resilience in the face of challenges can forge extraordinary character and insight. These stories remind us that genius often emerges not despite adversity but because of it, highlighting the transformative power of perseverance and grit.

A Practical Perspective: Cultivating Potential

For those seeking to unlock their own genius, the nature-versus-nurture debate offers both reassurance and responsibility. While natural abilities may vary from person to person, the nurturing of potential is a universal possibility. This realization invites us to shift the focus from inherent limitations to the opportunities we create for growth.

Practical strategies for cultivating genius begin with recognizing one's strengths and interests. Whether through formal education, self-directed learning, or hands-on experience, the key is to create an environment that encourages curiosity, experimentation, and resilience. Surrounding oneself with supportive mentors, collaborators, and resources can further amplify these efforts, enabling individuals to reach heights they might not achieve alone.

At the same time, embracing the challenges and setbacks inherent in any journey of growth is essential. As Edison, Franklin, and countless others have shown, the path to genius is rarely smooth. It is through perseverance, adaptability, and a willingness to learn from failure that extraordinary achievements become possible.

The Fusion of Potential and Practice

Ultimately, the question of whether genius is born or made becomes less important than understanding how the two forces interact. By embracing both our natural abilities and the opportunities to develop them, we can unlock new realms of possibility. Genius, then, is not an elusive trait reserved for the select few. It is a process—a dynamic and evolving journey that we all have the capacity to embark upon.

As we explore the remaining sections of this chapter and beyond, the lessons of history's greatest thinkers will continue to illuminate this path. Their lives remind us that while we may not all be born with the brilliance of Mozart or the resilience of Mandela, the potential for greatness lies within us all, waiting to be nurtured into fruition.

Awakening Your Inner Genius

Genius is often portrayed as an extraordinary gift possessed by a select few, an ethereal quality that feels distant from everyday experience. Yet, history and science tell a different story: genius is not a fixed trait but a potential that exists within all of us, waiting to be realized. Awakening this potential is not a matter of sudden revelation but of intentional cultivation. It requires a willingness to explore, experiment, and embrace the journey of self-discovery. This section offers a roadmap for recognizing and nurturing your inner genius, setting the stage for the transformative lessons ahead.

The Power of Self-Belief

The first step to awakening your inner genius is to believe it exists. Many of history's great thinkers and innovators began their journeys not with certainty, but with curiosity and self-trust. Albert Einstein, often regarded as the quintessential genius, struggled in school and was once dismissed as an underachiever. Yet he persisted, driven by an unwavering belief in his ability to explore the mysteries of the universe. His story reminds us that self-belief is the foundation upon which genius is built.

Self-belief does not mean blind confidence. Instead, it is the quiet assurance that growth is possible—a mindset that views challenges as opportunities rather than obstacles. Psychologist Carol Dweck's concept of the "growth mindset" encapsulates this principle. By embracing the idea that abilities can be developed through effort and learning, we create the conditions for our genius to emerge.

Curiosity as a Compass

At the heart of genius lies an insatiable curiosity—a hunger to understand, question, and explore. Leonardo da Vinci, whose contributions spanned art, science, and engineering, exemplified this trait. His notebooks, filled with sketches and musings on everything from anatomy to the flight of birds, reveal a mind constantly engaged with the world. For Da Vinci, curiosity was not a passive interest but an active pursuit, a way of seeing the world with fresh eyes.

Cultivating curiosity begins with asking better

questions. Instead of accepting things at face value, challenge yourself to dig deeper. Why does a particular phenomenon occur? How might it be applied in a new context? Engaging with the world in this way not only expands your knowledge but also opens the door to creative insights. Journaling, reading widely, and seeking diverse perspectives are practical ways to foster curiosity in your daily life.

Embracing the Art of Practice

While curiosity provides the spark, mastery comes through practice. The myth of the "effortless genius" is just that—a myth. Even prodigies like Mozart achieved greatness through years of dedicated effort. Modern research supports this idea, showing that deliberate practice—focused, goal-oriented repetition—is a critical factor in developing expertise.

To awaken your inner genius, identify a skill or area of interest you are passionate about and commit to deliberate practice. This involves breaking tasks into manageable components, seeking feedback, and continually refining your approach. Progress may be slow at first, but each step builds the neural connections that enable mastery over time. As the Japanese concept of *kaizen* teaches, small, consistent improvements lead to extraordinary results.

Creating an Environment for Genius

Genius does not thrive in isolation. It is shaped by the environments we inhabit and the people we surround ourselves with. Think of the "genius clusters" of history, from the intellectual vibrancy of Ancient Athens to the innovation hubs of Silicon Valley. These environments fostered creativity by providing opportunities for collaboration, mentorship, and inspiration.

You can create your own environment for genius by curating spaces that encourage focus and creativity. Whether it's a dedicated workspace, a network of like-minded individuals, or simply a routine that prioritizes deep work, the right environment can amplify your efforts. Surrounding yourself with people who challenge and inspire you is equally important. As Jim Rohn famously said, "You are the average of the five people you spend the most time with."

The Role of Resilience

No journey of growth is without setbacks, and the path to genius is no exception. Resilience— the ability to recover from difficulties and adapt to challenges—is a defining trait of extraordinary individuals. Thomas Edison's famous persistence in developing the light bulb, despite thousands of failed attempts, is a testament to the power of resilience. He viewed each failure not as a defeat but as a step closer to success.

To cultivate resilience, shift your perspective on failure. Instead of seeing it as an endpoint, recognize it as part of the learning process. Reflect on setbacks to identify what they teach you, and use that knowledge to refine your approach. Practices like mindfulness and journaling can also help you build emotional resilience, providing a stable foundation for growth.

Tapping into Flow

One of the most profound ways to access your inner genius is through the state of "flow." Coined by psychologist Mihaly Csikszentmihalyi, flow describes the experience of being fully immersed in a task, where time seems to disappear and performance reaches its peak. Athletes, artists, and scientists often report achieving their best work in this state.

Flow arises when challenge and skill are perfectly balanced—when the task is demanding enough to engage you but not so difficult as to overwhelm you. To cultivate flow, identify activities that align with your strengths and passions, and minimize distractions during periods of focused work. Developing rituals or routines that signal your brain to enter a state of focus can also enhance your ability to achieve flow.

A Call to Action

As we conclude this section, it's worth reflecting on the essence of genius: it is not a destination but a process, a way of engaging with the world that combines curiosity, effort, and resilience. The tools and techniques described here are not reserved for an elite few; they are accessible to anyone willing to embark on the journey of self-discovery and growth.

The chapters ahead will delve deeper into the

principles and practices that unlock genius, drawing on the wisdom of history's greatest minds. But the first step is yours to take. Begin by believing in your potential, cultivating curiosity, and embracing the art of practice. Genius, after all, is not about being extraordinary—it's about making the ordinary extraordinary through your approach, your mindset, and your actions.

CHAPTER 2: VISION AND IMAGINATION – THE SEEDS OF INNOVATION

The Role of Imagination in Historical Breakthroughs

Imagination is the silent architect of progress, an invisible force shaping the tangible world. It allows us to transcend the boundaries of the present, envisioning possibilities that seem impossible until they are realized. Throughout history, some of the most groundbreaking achievements have been fueled not by mere intellect or resources but by the audacity to imagine a world that could be different. Figures like Albert Einstein and Nikola Tesla epitomize this spirit, demonstrating how imagination serves as the wellspring of innovation and the precursor to execution.

Einstein's Thought Experiments: Imagining the Universe

Albert Einstein once remarked, "Imagination is more important than knowledge. For knowledge is limited, whereas imagination embraces the entire world." This belief was not just a philosophical musing but a guiding principle in his work. Einstein's revolutionary theories, including special and general relativity, were born not in laboratories but in the theater of his mind. He engaged in "thought experiments," a mental exercise where he envisioned scenarios that challenged conventional understanding.

One of his most famous thought experiments involved imagining himself riding alongside a beam of light. This visualization led him to question how time and space would behave under such circumstances. By mentally exploring these concepts, Einstein was able to develop theories that redefined our understanding of the universe. His ability to rely on imagination as a tool of inquiry demonstrates a profound truth: before something can be proven or built, it must first be conceived in the mind's eye.

Einstein's process offers a lesson for modern innovators. While technical skills and empirical data are essential, the capacity to think beyond what is known—to ask "what if?"—is equally critical. By allowing imagination to guide inquiry, we create the conditions for transformative ideas to emerge.

Tesla's Vision of the Future: A World Beyond Boundaries

If Einstein's genius lay in imagining the invisible forces of the cosmos, Nikola Tesla's brilliance was in envisioning a world electrified by his inventions. Tesla's ability to conceptualize his designs entirely in his mind, without the need for prototypes, was legendary. He referred to this process as "visualization," a practice that allowed him to construct, test, and refine complex systems mentally before bringing them to life.

One of Tesla's most ambitious visions was the idea of wireless energy transmission. He imagined a world where power could be distributed through the air, eliminating the need for wires and infrastructure. Though the technology to fully realize this dream was beyond his time, Tesla's visionary thinking laid the foundation for modern wireless communication, from Wi-Fi to cellular networks.

Tesla's story illustrates the power of imagination to transcend the limitations of the present. While his ideas were often dismissed as fantastical, they served as a beacon for future innovation. His life serves as a reminder that true visionaries are not constrained by what is

practical in the moment—they dare to dream of
what could be.

Imagination as the Driver of Progress

The stories of Einstein and Tesla highlight a critical aspect of imagination: its role as a driver of
progress. Without the ability to imagine alternative realities, humanity would remain confined
to its current circumstances. Imagination fuels
creativity, and creativity, in turn, leads to invention and discovery.

Consider the invention of the airplane by the
Wright brothers. Before flight was a reality, it
was a dream—a concept inspired by observing
birds and envisioning the possibility of human
flight. Similarly, the development of the internet
began as a vision of global connectivity, a way
to link people and ideas across vast distances. These breakthroughs remind us that imagination is not a passive exercise but an active
process of challenging norms and exploring
uncharted territory.

The link between imagination and progress
also extends to the arts and humanities. Writers,

artists, and musicians have used their creative visions to inspire social change and challenge cultural paradigms. Harriet Beecher Stowe's *Uncle Tom's Cabin* envisioned a world free of slavery, galvanizing the abolitionist movement. Pablo Picasso's *Guernica* captured the horrors of war, sparking conversations about the human cost of conflict. These examples demonstrate that imagination is not limited to technological innovation; it is the foundation of all human progress.

Cultivating Imagination in Daily Life

While the achievements of historical visionaries may seem distant from everyday experience, the ability to harness imagination is accessible to all. The first step is to create mental space for imagination to flourish. In a world dominated by deadlines, routines, and information overload, it is easy to lose touch with the creative mind. Yet, as Einstein's thought experiments and Tesla's visualizations show, moments of reflection and mental exploration are essential for cultivating imagination.

Engaging in creative activities — whether

through writing, drawing, or brainstorming—
can also stimulate the imagination. These practices encourage the mind to make connections
between seemingly unrelated ideas, sparking
new insights. Daydreaming, once dismissed as a
distraction, is now recognized by psychologists
as a powerful tool for creative problem-solving.
By allowing the mind to wander, we create opportunities for innovation to emerge.

The environment also plays a crucial role in
fostering imagination. Surrounding yourself
with diverse perspectives, engaging with art
and literature, and exposing yourself to new
experiences can expand your mental horizons.
The more varied the inputs, the richer the ideas
that imagination can generate.

The Responsibility of Visionaries

Imagination is a gift, but it is also a responsibility. The ability to envision the future carries with
it the obligation to act ethically and thoughtfully. Visionaries like Einstein and Tesla were not
only innovators but also advocates for using
their discoveries to benefit humanity. Einstein,
for instance, was deeply concerned about the

ethical implications of nuclear energy, while Tesla dreamed of a world where technology served the common good.

As we cultivate our own imagination, we must also consider the impact of our ideas. Will they contribute to progress and well-being, or will they perpetuate harm? This balance between creativity and responsibility is what separates mere dreamers from true visionaries.

A Path Forward

Imagination is the starting point of every great endeavor. It bridges the gap between the known and the unknown, transforming abstract ideas into concrete realities. By studying the lives of visionaries like Einstein and Tesla, we gain not only inspiration but also practical insights into how imagination can be cultivated and applied. As we move through the rest of this chapter, we will explore the challenges and opportunities that accompany visionary thinking, equipping ourselves to imagine—and create—a better future.

Barriers to Creativity

Creativity is often romanticized as a boundless force, an untamed energy that flows freely in the minds of visionaries. Yet, for most people, creativity feels anything but effortless. Barriers—both internal and external—can stifle the imagination, leaving even the most inspired minds feeling constrained. To unlock the full potential of visionary thinking, it is essential to understand these barriers, confront them, and cultivate an environment where creativity can thrive.

The Fear of Failure: Creativity's Most Persistent Enemy

One of the most pervasive barriers to creativity is the fear of failure. This fear, deeply ingrained in human psychology, can paralyze the imagination and prevent individuals from taking the risks necessary for innovation. Thomas Edison's famous quip—"I have not failed. I've just found 10,000 ways that won't work"—highlights an essential truth about creativity: failure is an inevitable part of the process.

Despite this, societal pressures often amplify the fear of failure. In educational systems, workplaces, and social settings, mistakes are frequently stigmatized rather than celebrated as opportunities for growth. This creates a culture of perfectionism, where individuals are reluctant to experiment or share ideas that might not succeed. For creative breakthroughs to occur, it is crucial to reframe failure as a learning experience rather than a final verdict.

Overcoming Fear: Lessons from Frida Kahlo

Frida Kahlo, one of the most iconic artists of the 20th century, exemplifies how creativity can flourish in the face of adversity and fear. Kahlo's life was marked by immense physical pain and emotional turmoil, yet she used these struggles as fuel for her art. Her deeply personal and often unconventional works challenged societal norms and redefined artistic expression.

Kahlo's story demonstrates that overcoming the fear of failure requires courage and vulnerability. Creativity thrives not in the absence of fear but in the willingness to confront it. By embracing imperfection and allowing ourselves to take risks, we create the conditions for true innovation to emerge.

The Conformity Trap: When Rules Replace Vision

Another significant barrier to creativity is con-formity—the pressure to adhere to established norms and expectations. From an early age, in-dividuals are often taught to prioritize structure and compliance over exploration and original-ity. While rules and frameworks serve import-ant functions, they can also become constraints, limiting the scope of what is possible.

Consider the story of Galileo Galilei, the pio-neering scientist who challenged the orthodoxy of his time. By questioning the prevailing geo-centric model of the universe, Galileo opened the door to a revolutionary understanding of planetary motion. His willingness to defy con-vention and embrace controversy underscores a critical aspect of creativity: the ability to see beyond accepted paradigms.

For modern readers, breaking free from confor-mity requires cultivating a mindset of curiosity and independent thought. This does not mean rejecting all rules but rather questioning whether those rules serve progress or perpetuate stagnation. By remaining open to new perspectives and challenging assumptions, we create the space for visionary ideas to take root.

The Noise of Distraction: Creativity in a Digital Age

In today's hyperconnected world, one of the most insidious barriers to creativity is distraction. The constant influx of notifications, emails, and social media updates fragments attention, leaving little room for the sustained focus required for deep, imaginative thinking. Research has shown that multitasking not only reduces productivity but also inhibits creative problem-solving by preventing the brain from entering a state of flow.

Nikola Tesla, known for his singular focus and imaginative brilliance, offers a stark contrast to this modern challenge. Tesla often worked in solitude, immersing himself in his thoughts and visualizing his inventions with remarkable clarity. This ability to disconnect from external distractions allowed him to channel his creativity into groundbreaking innovations.

For those seeking to cultivate creativity in the digital age, the lesson is clear: create intentional spaces for focus and reflection. Whether through mindfulness practices, designated tech-free periods, or immersive creative sessions, reducing distractions can help unlock the full potential of the imagination.

The Scarcity of Play: Creativity's Forgotten Ally

Playfulness, often dismissed as frivolous, is one of the most powerful catalysts for creativity. Albert Einstein famously credited his breakthroughs to a childlike sense of wonder, a quality that allowed him to approach complex problems with curiosity and openness. Yet, as adults, many of us lose touch with this playful mindset, replacing it with rigid routines and relentless productivity.

The scarcity of play is not merely a personal issue but a cultural one. Societal values that prioritize efficiency and measurable outcomes often leave little room for exploration and experimentation. This focus on output over process stifles the imagination, turning creative endeavors into mechanical tasks rather than joyful pursuits.

Reclaiming a sense of play involves giving ourselves permission to experiment without immediate goals or expectations. Whether through hobbies, improvisation, or simply daydreaming, play fosters the kind of open-ended thinking that leads to creative breakthroughs. By embracing a playful approach to challenges, we tap into a wellspring of ideas that might otherwise remain dormant.

The Shadow of Self-Doubt

Perhaps the most personal and pervasive barrier to creativity is self-doubt—the inner critic that questions our worth and capabilities. This voice, often amplified by external judgment, can erode confidence and prevent individuals from pursuing their ideas. Even luminaries like Vincent van Gogh grappled with profound self-doubt, yet their willingness to persevere in the face of uncertainty underscores an essential truth: creativity requires resilience.

Overcoming self-doubt begins with recognizing its presence and challenging its validity. Practices like affirmations, journaling, and seeking supportive communities can help quiet the inner critic and create a more nurturing mental environment. By acknowledging our doubts without allowing them to define us, we build the confidence to share our ideas and explore our creative potential.

Creating a Path Forward

Understanding the barriers to creativity is the first step to overcoming them. Whether it is fear, conformity, distraction, or self-doubt, each obstacle offers an opportunity for growth and transformation. By addressing these barriers with intention and resilience, we create the conditions for visionary thinking to flourish.

As we continue this chapter, we will explore practical strategies for cultivating a visionary mindset, drawing on the lessons of history's great thinkers and innovators. Creativity, as these stories remind us, is not a gift bestowed upon a select few—it is a practice, a process, and a way of engaging with the world. The seeds of innovation lie within each of us, waiting to be nurtured into fruition.

Cultivating a Visionary Mindset

Visionary thinking is not a mysterious gift bestowed upon a chosen few—it is a skill that can be cultivated, nurtured, and refined. While the spark of inspiration may strike unexpectedly, the ability to sustain and act upon that vision comes from deliberate practice. By adopting habits and exercises that enhance creative thinking, we can develop a mindset capable of imagining transformative ideas and turning them into reality.

The Foundation: Embracing Curiosity and Openness

At the heart of a visionary mindset lies curiosity—the insatiable desire to learn, question, and explore. Leonardo da Vinci, one of history's most celebrated polymaths, exemplified this quality. His notebooks reveal a relentless curiosity about the world, from the mechanics of flight to the anatomy of the human body. Da Vinci's genius was not confined to any single field; it was fueled by an openness to new ideas and an eagerness to connect seemingly unrelated concepts.

To cultivate this level of curiosity, start by asking questions about the world around you. Why do things work the way they do? What possibilities lie beyond the obvious? Reading widely, engaging with diverse perspectives, and exposing yourself to new experiences can further ignite your curiosity. The key is to approach life with a beginner's mindset, free of assumptions and preconceptions.

Creative Visualization: Imagining the Possibilities

One of the most powerful tools for cultivating a visionary mindset is creative visualization—the practice of imagining desired outcomes with clarity and detail. Nikola Tesla was a master of this technique, often constructing his inventions entirely in his mind before bringing them to life. Visualization allowed Tesla to test and refine his ideas without the constraints of physical resources, enabling him to innovate with remarkable efficiency.

To practice creative visualization, set aside time each day to imagine a goal or challenge you wish to address. Close your eyes and picture the details as vividly as possible: the sights, sounds, and sensations associated with success. This exercise not only enhances your ability to think imaginatively but also helps align your actions with your vision, creating a sense of purpose and direction.

The Power of "What If" Thinking

Visionaries often approach challenges with a simple yet profound question: "What if?" This question opens the door to creative possibilities, allowing the mind to explore alternative realities and solutions. Einstein's thought experiments, where he imagined riding on a beam of light or observing clocks from different perspectives, were rooted in this type of thinking.

You can incorporate "What if" thinking into your daily routine by challenging conventional assumptions. What if a process could be simplified? What if a product could serve an entirely new purpose? By reframing problems as opportunities for exploration, you begin to see potential where others see limitations.

Creating a Space for Imagination

Environment plays a crucial role in fostering visionary thinking. Just as a garden needs sunlight and water to thrive, the mind requires a supportive space to nurture its creative potential. Virginia Woolf famously wrote about the need for "a room of one's own" — a quiet space where ideas can flourish free from distraction.

Designing such a space doesn't require grandeur; it can be as simple as a corner of your home or a favorite spot in nature. What matters is that it offers an atmosphere conducive to reflection and focus. Fill this space with tools that inspire you, whether they are books, art supplies, or a journal. The goal is to create an environment where your imagination feels unbounded.

Collaboration as a Catalyst

While solitude is valuable, collaboration can also

serve as a powerful catalyst for visionary thinking. History is filled with examples of breakthroughs that emerged from dynamic partnerships, from the Wright brothers' invention of the airplane to the creative synergy between Steve Jobs and Steve Wozniak. Collaboration allows individuals to build upon one another's ideas, leading to innovations that might not have been possible alone.

To foster collaborative creativity, seek out diverse perspectives and engage in meaningful dialogue with others. This might involve joining a mastermind group, participating in creative workshops, or simply brainstorming with friends and colleagues. The key is to approach collaboration with an open mind, valuing the unique contributions of others while remaining true to your own vision.

Overcoming Creative Blocks

Even the most visionary thinkers encounter moments of stagnation, where ideas seem elusive and progress feels out of reach. These creative blocks are a natural part of the process, but they can be overcome with intentional strategies. One such technique is "mind mapping," a visual method of organizing thoughts and generating new connections. By starting with a central idea and branching out into related concepts, you can uncover patterns and insights that might otherwise go unnoticed.

Another effective approach is to take a break and engage in a completely different activity. This allows the subconscious mind to continue processing the problem, often leading to sudden "aha" moments. Many visionaries, including Einstein and Beethoven, credited their break-throughs to moments of relaxation and play, underscoring the importance of balance in the creative process.

Building Resilience and Persistence

A visionary mindset is not just about generating ideas—it is about seeing them through to fruition. This requires resilience and persistence, particularly in the face of setbacks and skepticism. Thomas Edison's tenacity in pursuing the invention of the light bulb, despite numerous failures, serves as a powerful reminder of the importance of perseverance.

To build resilience, focus on the intrinsic value of your creative pursuits rather than external validation. Celebrate small victories along the way, and view challenges as opportunities to refine your ideas. By maintaining a long-term perspective, you can stay motivated even when progress feels slow.

The Daily Practice of Visionary Thinking

Cultivating a visionary mindset is not a one-time effort but a daily practice. Set aside time each day to engage in activities that stimulate your imagination, whether it's journaling, sketching, or brainstorming. Reflect on your goals and aspirations, and allow yourself to dream boldly without fear of judgment.

As you integrate these practices into your life, you will begin to notice subtle shifts in the way you approach challenges and opportunities. Ideas that once seemed out of reach will start to take shape, and the barriers to creativity will give way to a sense of possibility.

A Mindset for Transformation

Visionary thinking is not a destination—it is a journey, a way of seeing the world through the lens of possibility and innovation. By embracing curiosity, practicing visualization, and creating environments that nurture creativity, you can unlock the full potential of your imagination. As we explore the final section of this chapter, we will examine how visionary thinking has transformed industries, communities, and lives, offering inspiration for what is possible when we dare to dream.

The Modern Application of Vision

Visionary thinking is not confined to history; it is a living force that continues to shape the world around us. From technological advancements to artistic revolutions and transformative leadership, the application of vision today is more important than ever. In a rapidly changing landscape, those who dare to imagine new possibilities and act upon them become the architects of progress. This section explores how visionary thinking manifests in contemporary society, inspiring readers to harness its power in their own lives.

Technology: Envisioning a Connected Future

Few realms illustrate the impact of visionary thinking more vividly than technology. Consider the story of Steve Jobs, whose ability to imagine the intersection of technology and humanity transformed the way we interact with the world. Jobs did not merely see the personal computer as a machine; he envisioned it as an extension of the human experience. This vision led to the creation of groundbreaking products like the iPhone, which revolutionized communication, commerce, and creativity.

The essence of Jobs' visionary thinking lay in his ability to anticipate needs that people had not yet articulated. He famously remarked, "People don't know what they want until you show it to them." This principle reflects a critical aspect of visionary application: the capacity to see beyond immediate demands and imagine possibilities that redefine the future.

Today, technological visionaries continue to push boundaries in areas like artificial intelligence, renewable energy, and space exploration.

Elon Musk, for example, envisions a multi-planetary existence for humanity through SpaceX, while simultaneously revolutionizing transportation with Tesla. These endeavors exemplify how visionary thinking can tackle some of the world's most pressing challenges, offering inspiration for others to pursue bold ideas.

Art: Pioneering New Frontiers of Expression

Visionary thinking is not limited to science and technology; it also fuels artistic innovation, providing new ways to interpret and experience the world. Contemporary artists like Ai Weiwei use their vision to challenge societal norms and provoke critical dialogue. Ai's installations, often addressing themes of freedom and human rights, demonstrate how art can transcend aesthetic boundaries to engage with broader cultural and political issues.

Similarly, the rise of digital art and virtual reality has opened new frontiers for creative expression. Visionaries in this space, such as Beeple, have embraced blockchain technology to create and distribute art in unprecedented ways. Beeple's record-breaking NFT sale not only redefined the value of digital art but also challenged traditional perceptions of ownership and creativity.

These examples highlight a core tenet of visionary thinking in the arts: the courage to challenge conventions and imagine new possibilities. For readers seeking to apply this principle in their own lives, the lesson is clear: creativity thrives at the intersection of tradition and innovation, where bold experimentation leads to transformative outcomes.

Leadership: Guiding with Purpose and Vision

In leadership, visionary thinking serves as a compass, guiding individuals and organizations toward meaningful goals. Great leaders do not simply react to circumstances; they anticipate change, articulate a compelling vision, and inspire others to join them on the journey. Consider Martin Luther King Jr., whose dream of racial equality transcended the constraints of his time and galvanized a movement that reshaped society.

Modern leadership continues to be defined by

visionaries who prioritize purpose over prof-
it. Jacinda Ardern, the Prime Minister of New
Zealand, has been widely praised for her empathetic and forward-thinking approach to governance. Her leadership during crises, from the
Christchurch mosque shootings to the COVID-
19 pandemic, demonstrates the power of a clear
and compassionate vision in fostering resilience
and unity.

For readers aspiring to lead with vision, these
examples underscore the importance of clarity,
authenticity, and the ability to inspire others.
Visionary leaders are not afraid to take risks or
challenge the status quo; they understand that
progress often requires bold and unconventional thinking.

**Practical Applications for Everyday Visionar-
ies**

While the achievements of visionaries like Jobs,
Musk, and Ardern may seem extraordinary, the
principles of visionary thinking can be applied
in everyday life. Vision begins with a mindset—
an openness to possibilities and a willingness
to question assumptions. By integrating this

mindset into daily habits, anyone can cultivate the capacity to imagine and act upon transformative ideas.

One practical approach is to set aside time for "blue-sky thinking," where you allow yourself to dream without limitations. This exercise encourages you to think beyond immediate constraints and explore long-term possibilities. Whether you are envisioning a new career path, a creative project, or a solution to a persistent challenge, this practice can help you clarify your goals and generate innovative ideas.

Another strategy is to embrace collaboration and seek diverse perspectives. Just as leaders like Ardern prioritize inclusivity, engaging with people from different backgrounds and disciplines can broaden your vision and reveal opportunities you might not have considered. This approach not only enhances creativity but also fosters a sense of shared purpose, empowering you to turn vision into action.

The Responsibility of Visionaries in a Changing World

As we navigate the complexities of the modern world, the need for visionary thinking has never been greater. Climate change, social inequality, and technological disruption present challenges that require innovative and inclusive solutions. Visionaries have a unique responsibility to use their imagination and influence for the greater good, balancing ambition with ethical considerations.

This responsibility is evident in the growing emphasis on sustainability and social impact across industries. Companies like Patagonia have demonstrated how visionary thinking can align profitability with environmental stewardship, inspiring a new generation of conscious entrepreneurs. Similarly, movements like Black Lives Matter illustrate the power of grassroots visionaries to drive systemic change through collective action.

For readers, these examples serve as a reminder that visionary thinking is not only about personal achievement but also about contributing to a better world. By aligning your vision with values that prioritize equity, sustainability, and human dignity, you can make a meaningful impact in your community and beyond.

A Call to Action

The modern application of vision is a testament to the enduring power of imagination and innovation. Whether in technology, art, or leadership, the ability to envision a better future and take action is what distinguishes the extraordinary from the ordinary. As we conclude this chapter, let these stories and principles inspire you to embrace your own visionary potential.

Visionary thinking is not reserved for a select few—it is a practice that can be cultivated through curiosity, resilience, and a commitment to progress. By applying these principles in your own life, you can become an agent of change, transforming challenges into opportunities and ideas into reality. The seeds of innovation are within you; the time to plant them is now.

CHAPTER 3: MASTERY THROUGH FOCUS – THE POWER OF DEEP WORK

The Art of Sustained Focus

In a world driven by speed and multitasking, the ability to sustain focus has become a rare and invaluable skill. Yet, history reminds us that some of humanity's greatest achievements were born not from haste but from patient, unwavering dedication. The art of sustained focus—of immersing oneself so deeply in a task that the world fades away—has shaped masterpieces, scientific breakthroughs, and innovations that have stood the test of time. By examining historical examples, we can uncover timeless lessons on the power of deep work and its potential to transform our own lives.

Michelangelo and the Sistine Chapel: A Testament to Tenacity

Few stories illustrate the power of sustained focus more vividly than that of Michelangelo and the Sistine Chapel ceiling. Commissioned in 1508 by Pope Julius II, the project presented immense challenges. Michelangelo, known primarily as a sculptor at the time, was reluctant to take on the monumental task of painting. The ceiling's vast surface spanned over 5,000 square feet and required the creation of more than 300 intricate figures, each imbued with dynamic energy and profound meaning.

For four years, Michelangelo worked tirelessly, often lying on scaffolding for hours on end, painting with his arms outstretched above him. The physical toll was immense; he endured chronic back and neck pain and the constant discomfort of paint dripping into his eyes. Yet, he persisted, driven by a singular focus on the vision he sought to bring to life. The result was a masterpiece that redefined Renaissance art and continues to inspire awe centuries later.

Michelangelo's story offers a profound lesson: mastery requires more than talent—it demands discipline, perseverance, and the ability to sustain focus in the face of adversity. His dedication reminds us that the path to greatness is rarely easy, but the rewards of deep work are enduring and transformative.

Newton's Years of Isolation: Focus in the Midst of Crisis

Another remarkable example of sustained focus

comes from the life of Isaac Newton. In 1665, the Great Plague swept through England, forcing Newton to retreat to his family estate in Woolsthorpe. While this period of isolation disrupted normal life for many, it became one of the most productive phases in Newton's career. Freed from the distractions of university life, he devoted himself entirely to his studies.

During this time, Newton developed foundational theories that would change the course of science, including his work on calculus, optics, and the laws of motion. The story of the falling apple, which inspired his theory of gravity, is emblematic of the clarity and insight that can emerge from focused reflection.

Newton's example underscores the value of creating space for deep thinking, even in the midst of chaos. By carving out time to immerse ourselves in meaningful work, we can unlock insights and achievements that might otherwise remain elusive.

The Japanese Concept of "Shokunin": Focus as a Way of Life

The art of sustained focus is not limited to grand historical figures; it is also deeply rooted in cultural traditions. In Japan, the concept of *shokunin* embodies the pursuit of mastery through unwavering dedication to one's craft. A *shokunin* is not merely a craftsman but an artist and perfectionist who approaches their work with a sense of purpose and reverence.

Consider the work of Jiro Ono, the renowned sushi chef featured in the documentary *Jiro Dreams of Sushi*. At the age of 85, Jiro continued to refine his craft, striving for perfection in every dish. His approach exemplifies the *shokunin* spirit: a commitment to focus, discipline, and continuous improvement.

The philosophy of *shokunin* teaches us that sustained focus is not only about achieving monumental accomplishments but also about finding meaning and fulfillment in the pursuit of excellence. By applying this mindset to our own work, no matter how ordinary it may seem, we can elevate our efforts and create something truly remarkable.

Practical Lessons for Modern Life

While the stories of Michelangelo, Newton, and Jiro Ono may seem distant from contemporary experience, their lessons are deeply relevant to modern challenges. In a world filled with distractions, the ability to focus has become both a rare skill and a competitive advantage. Yet, focus is not an innate quality—it is a discipline that can be cultivated through intentional practice.

One way to begin is by identifying tasks that require deep work and setting aside dedicated time for them. This might involve creating a daily ritual, such as working on a project during the early morning hours when the mind is most alert. Eliminating distractions, whether by turning off notifications or finding a quiet space, can also help create an environment conducive to focus.

Another important practice is to embrace the discomfort that often accompanies sustained effort. Just as Michelangelo endured physical strain and Newton wrestled with complex ideas, we must be willing to persevere through the challenges that arise during deep work. This resilience not only enhances our capacity for focus but also builds the mental fortitude needed to tackle ambitious goals.

A Call to Embrace Deep Work

The art of sustained focus is not about achieving perfection—it is about committing to the process of growth and discovery. Whether we are painting a masterpiece, solving a scientific puzzle, or simply striving to do our best in everyday tasks, the principles of deep work remain the same: clarity of purpose, disciplined effort, and a willingness to immerse ourselves fully in the moment.

As we explore the remaining sections of this chapter, we will delve into the challenges of maintaining focus in a distracted world and the strategies that can help us reclaim our attention. The lessons of history's great achievers remind us that the power of sustained focus is within our grasp, waiting to be harnessed for the pursuit of our own aspirations.

The Challenges of Modern Distractions

In the golden age of connectivity, distraction has become an omnipresent force, eroding our ability to concentrate and undermining our potential for deep, focused work. While technology has unlocked unprecedented opportunities, it has also fragmented our attention, replacing moments of stillness with endless notifications and multitasking. This environment poses a stark challenge: how can we cultivate focus in a world designed to scatter it?

The Illusion of Multitasking

At the heart of the modern focus crisis lies the myth of multitasking—the belief that we can juggle multiple tasks simultaneously without compromising productivity or quality. Neuroscience, however, tells a different story. The brain does not truly multitask; instead, it engages in "task switching," rapidly toggling between activities. Each switch imposes a cognitive cost, reducing efficiency and increasing mental fatigue.

Consider the workplace scenario of writing an important report while responding to emails and instant messages. Each interruption forces the brain to recalibrate, disrupting the flow of thought and diminishing the depth of engagement. Over time, this pattern not only reduces the quality of work but also fosters a sense of perpetual busyness without meaningful accomplishment.

The dangers of multitasking extend beyond productivity. Studies have shown that frequent task switching impairs memory, reduces creativity, and heightens stress levels. In an age where attention has become a currency, the ability to focus on a single task may be one of the most valuable skills we can develop.

The Role of Technology: A Double-Edged Sword

Technology, with its promise of convenience and efficiency, is both a blessing and a curse. Tools like smartphones, social media, and collaborative platforms have revolutionized communication and information sharing, but they have also introduced a relentless stream of interruptions. The average smartphone user checks their device over 150 times a day, often driven by the compulsion to respond to notifications or scroll through endless feeds.

This constant engagement with technology alters the brain's reward system, creating a feedback loop of distraction. Each notification triggers a surge of dopamine, a neurotransmitter associated with pleasure and reward. Over time, the brain becomes conditioned to seek these short bursts of gratification, prioritizing them over sustained effort and long-term goals.

The impact of this digital dependence extends beyond individuals to society at large. A culture of immediacy has emerged, where the value of deep, reflective work is overshadowed by the allure of instant responses and real-time updates. For those seeking mastery, this cultural shift poses a significant obstacle, demanding intentional strategies to reclaim focus.

The Cognitive Cost of a Distracted Mind

The effects of modern distractions are not merely behavioral—they are neurological. Research has shown that constant interruptions and multitasking physically alter the brain, weakening its ability to sustain attention. The prefrontal cortex, responsible for executive functions like decision-making and focus, becomes less efficient when subjected to chronic distractions.

Over time, this diminished capacity for focus can lead to what neuroscientists call "attention residue." This phenomenon occurs when fragments of a previous task linger in the mind, reducing the mental bandwidth available for the next task. Attention residue explains why transitioning between activities, such as moving from a meeting to a creative project, often feels mentally exhausting and unproductive.

In this context, the ability to enter a state of deep work—where the mind is fully immersed in a single, meaningful task—becomes increasingly elusive. Yet, as history's great achievers have shown, it is precisely this level of focus that enables extraordinary accomplishments.

The Loss of Flow: A Hidden Cost of Distraction

One of the most profound consequences of modern distractions is the loss of flow—a state of optimal engagement where time seems to disappear and performance reaches its peak. Psychologist Mihaly Csikszentmihalyi, who coined the term, described flow as the intersection of challenge and skill, where the mind is fully absorbed in the task at hand.

Distractions disrupt the delicate balance required to enter flow, fragmenting attention and pulling the mind away from deep engagement. For creatives, scientists, and professionals, this loss represents more than a missed opportunity; it is a barrier to achieving the breakthroughs and insights that define mastery.

Flow is not merely a byproduct of focus—it is a gateway to transformative work. Reclaiming this state requires not only minimizing distractions but also cultivating the discipline and intentionality needed to sustain concentration.

Overcoming the Challenges of a Distracted World

While the challenges of modern distractions may seem insurmountable, they are not beyond our control. History offers a guiding light, reminding us that focus is a skill that can be honed through deliberate effort and practice. Newton, Michelangelo, and other figures who achieved greatness did so by creating environments and routines that prioritized deep work.

In our own lives, this might mean setting boundaries with technology, such as designating tech-free periods or using apps to block distractions during focused work sessions. It could involve cultivating mindfulness practices, like meditation, to strengthen the brain's capacity for sustained attention. Ultimately, overcoming distraction requires a mindset shift: viewing focus not as a passive state but as an active, intentional choice.

A Call to Reclaim Focus

In a world increasingly dominated by noise, the ability to focus is not just a skill—it is an act of resistance. By acknowledging the challenges posed by modern distractions and taking intentional steps to address them, we can reclaim the mental clarity needed to pursue our most meaningful goals. As the next sections of this chapter will explore, the rewards of deep work are profound, offering not only increased productivity but also a sense of purpose and fulfillment that transcends the fleeting gratification of distraction.

Building the Discipline of Deep Work

Mastery is not an accident; it is a deliberate pursuit that requires focus, effort, and structure. In a world filled with distractions, the ability to engage in deep work—the concentrated effort on a cognitively demanding task—has become a superpower. Yet, the discipline required for deep work does not come naturally; it must be cultivated through intentional practices and a supportive environment. By drawing lessons from history's great thinkers and applying proven techniques, we can build the habits and mindset necessary to unlock our full potential.

Creating a Sanctuary for Focus

Environment shapes behavior. Just as a sculptor requires a well-equipped studio and a writer needs a quiet desk, deep work demands a space free from distractions. Virginia Woolf's concept of "a room of one's own" resonates deeply here: a physical and mental space dedicated to uninterrupted focus can transform the way we work.

Consider the example of Carl Jung, the famed psychologist who sought refuge from the distractions of his busy professional life by retreating to a stone tower he built in Bollingen, Switzerland. There, surrounded by nature and silence, Jung engaged in some of his most profound and creative thinking. The Bollingen Tower became his sanctuary for deep work, a space where he could explore ideas without interference.

For modern readers, creating such a sanctuary does not necessarily require a remote tower. It could be as simple as designating a specific room, desk, or corner for focused work. The key is consistency—when you repeatedly associate a space with deep work, it becomes easier to transition into a state of flow whenever you enter that environment.

The Power of Rituals and Routines

Rituals and routines are the scaffolding of discipline. By establishing a consistent approach to work, we reduce the cognitive effort required to get started and signal to our minds that it's time to focus. Beethoven, for instance, had a strict routine that included walking in nature each morning to generate ideas, followed by dedicated hours of composition. This ritual allowed him to harness both inspiration and structure in his creative process.

To build your own ritual for deep work, start by identifying a time of day when your energy and focus are at their peak. For many, this might be the early morning hours, before the demands of the day intrude. Establish a sequence of actions—such as brewing coffee, organizing your workspace, or reviewing your goals—that prepare your mind for concentrated effort. Over time, these rituals become a powerful cue for focus, easing the transition into deep work.

The Role of Boundaries and "Monastic" Focus

One of the most effective ways to cultivate deep work is to adopt what computer scientist and author Cal Newport calls a "monastic" approach to focus. This involves creating firm boundaries around your time and attention, shielding them from the distractions of email, social media, and other interruptions.

A historical example of this principle can be found in the work habits of mathematician Andrew Wiles. Wiles spent years in near-isolation while solving Fermat's Last Theorem, one of the most challenging problems in mathematics. By disconnecting from external distractions and dedicating himself entirely to the problem, he achieved a breakthrough that had eluded mathematicians for centuries.

For those unable to retreat into isolation, setting boundaries might involve simple practices such as scheduling specific times for checking messages or using apps to block digital distractions during focused work sessions. These small acts of discipline create the mental clarity needed to dive deeply into complex tasks.

Training the Mind: The Practice of Mindfulness

Building the discipline of deep work is not solely about managing the external environment; it also requires cultivating inner calm and focus. Mindfulness—the practice of bringing one's attention fully to the present moment—is a powerful tool for training the mind to resist distractions.

Historical figures such as the Stoic philosopher Marcus Aurelius recognized the value of mindfulness in achieving clarity and focus. In his *Meditations*, Aurelius often reflected on the importance of directing one's attention to the task at hand and remaining undisturbed by external noise. Similarly, modern mindfulness practices, such as meditation or deep breathing exercises, can help develop the mental resilience needed for deep work.

A practical way to integrate mindfulness into your routine is to begin each work session with a few moments of intentional breathing or reflection. This practice not only calms the mind but also reinforces your commitment to focus, creating a foundation for sustained effort.

The Role of Rest and Recovery

Deep work is demanding, and sustaining it requires balance. Just as athletes incorporate rest into their training schedules to allow for recovery and growth, those engaged in deep work must prioritize periods of rest to maintain productivity and creativity.

The concept of deliberate rest, explored by Alex Pang in his book *Rest: Why You Get More Done When You Work Less*, highlights the symbiotic relationship between focused effort and intentional downtime. Historical examples abound: Charles Darwin structured his days to include both focused scientific work and leisurely walks, while Winston Churchill famously took daily naps to recharge his mental energy.

Incorporating rest into your routine might involve short breaks during work sessions, extended periods of relaxation in the evenings, or activities that engage different parts of the brain, such as exercise or creative hobbies. These practices not only replenish energy but also provide the mental space needed for insights to emerge.

Embracing Progress Over Perfection

Finally, building the discipline of deep work requires letting go of perfectionism. The pursuit of mastery is a journey, and each focused session—no matter how imperfect—contributes to long-term growth. The writer Ernest Hemingway exemplified this principle, often emphasizing the importance of showing up and putting words on the page, even if the day's work was far from perfect.

For those cultivating deep work, the lesson is clear: consistency matters more than flawless execution. By committing to regular practice and celebrating incremental progress, we create the momentum needed to achieve our most ambitious goals.

A Blueprint for Discipline

The discipline of deep work is not an innate talent; it is a skill that can be developed through intentional effort and thoughtful strategies. By creating environments that foster focus, establishing rituals that prime the mind, and embracing rest as an integral part of the process, we can unlock the transformative power of deep work.

As the final section of this chapter will explore, the rewards of this discipline are profound, offering not only greater productivity but also a deeper sense of purpose and fulfillment. The path to mastery begins with a single step: the choice to focus, deeply and deliberately, on what truly matters.

The Rewards of Mastery

The pursuit of mastery through focus is not merely an exercise in discipline—it is a transformative journey that reshapes how we approach our work, relationships, and sense of purpose. When we dedicate ourselves to deep, concentrated effort, we unlock rewards that extend far beyond productivity. Mastery offers a profound sense of achievement, fulfillment, and clarity, reminding us of what it means to fully engage with life's most meaningful pursuits.

The Satisfaction of Excellence

At the heart of mastery lies the satisfaction of doing something exceptionally well. This sense of excellence is not limited to monumental achievements; it can be found in any endeavor approached with care and dedication. Consider the story of Yo-Yo Ma, one of the greatest cellists of our time. While his technical skill is unmatched, it is his commitment to continually refining his craft that sets him apart. In interviews, Ma often speaks of his deep connection to the music, a bond that emerges only through hours of focused practice and exploration.

For Ma, the reward of mastery is not only the accolades or public performances but also the personal fulfillment that comes from achieving a level of understanding and expression that transcends technique. This intrinsic reward is available to anyone who commits to mastering their chosen field or skill. Whether we are crafting a piece of art, solving a complex problem, or mentoring others, the process of striving for excellence enriches both the work and the individual.

Mastery as a Gateway to Innovation

Deep work and mastery do more than refine existing skills—they pave the way for innovation. History is filled with examples of breakthroughs that emerged only after years of concentrated effort. Consider the story of Marie Curie, who spent countless hours in her laboratory isolating radioactive elements. Her perseverance not only earned her two Nobel Prizes but also revolutionized science and medicine.

Mastery creates the foundation for creative leaps by deepening our understanding of a subject. When we immerse ourselves in a field, we begin to see connections and possibilities that others might overlook. This principle applies not only to scientific discoveries but also to artistic and entrepreneurial pursuits. Steve Jobs, for instance, often credited his mastery of design and technology with enabling him to reimagine products that would shape the modern world.

For readers seeking to unlock their own innovative potential, the lesson is clear: mastery is not an endpoint but a starting point. By dedicating ourselves to deep work, we cultivate the expertise and insight needed to push boundaries and create something truly original.

The Joy of Flow

One of the most profound rewards of mastery is the experience of flow—a state of complete immersion in an activity where time seems to dissolve and the mind operates at its peak. Psychologist Mihaly Csikszentmihalyi, who popularized the concept, described flow as a harmonious state where challenge and skill are perfectly balanced. This experience is not only deeply satisfying but also highly productive, enabling individuals to achieve their best work.

Flow often emerges when we engage in tasks that demand focus and stretch our abilities. Athletes, musicians, writers, and scientists frequently describe moments of flow as the highlight of their work, a feeling of being fully alive and attuned to their purpose. For example, Serena Williams has spoken about the sense of clarity and focus she experiences during high-stakes matches—a mental state honed through years of practice and mastery.

Cultivating flow requires creating the conditions for deep work: minimizing distractions, setting clear goals, and fully committing to the task at hand. As we build the discipline of focus, we increase our capacity to enter this state more frequently, enhancing both the quality of our work and our overall well-being.

The Impact on Personal Growth

The rewards of mastery extend beyond external achievements to foster profound personal growth. When we commit to mastering a skill or discipline, we cultivate traits such as resilience, patience, and adaptability. These qualities, developed through the challenges of deep work, become assets in every aspect of life.

Consider the journey of J.K. Rowling, who faced numerous rejections before publishing the first *Harry Potter* book. Her dedication to storytelling, despite setbacks, not only led to immense success but also demonstrated the transformative power of perseverance. Rowling's story reminds us that mastery is not about avoiding failure but about using it as a stepping stone to growth.

As we strive for mastery, we also deepen our understanding of ourselves—our strengths, limitations, and passions. This self-awareness enriches our relationships, careers, and sense of purpose, offering rewards that transcend any specific accomplishment.

Mastery's Ripple Effect: Inspiring Others

The pursuit of mastery is not a solitary endeavor; its impact often extends to others, inspiring and uplifting those around us. Teachers, leaders, and innovators who dedicate themselves to their craft often leave a lasting legacy, shaping the lives of those they influence. Consider Maya Angelou, whose mastery of language and storytelling not only earned her acclaim but also inspired millions to find their voice and pursue their dreams.

In our own lives, the ripple effect of mastery can manifest in subtle but meaningful ways. By modeling dedication, focus, and resilience, we encourage others to embrace their potential and strive for their own goals. Whether as parents, mentors, or colleagues, the pursuit of mastery allows us to contribute to a culture of growth and excellence.

The Fulfillment of Purpose

Ultimately, the greatest reward of mastery is the fulfillment that comes from aligning our efforts with our purpose. When we engage deeply with meaningful work, we experience a sense of connection and contribution that transcends individual achievement. This alignment with purpose is what gives mastery its transformative power, turning ordinary tasks into extraordinary experiences.

Victor Frankl, the renowned psychologist and Holocaust survivor, wrote in *Man's Search for Meaning* about the importance of purpose in overcoming life's challenges. While his circumstances were unimaginably difficult, his insights resonate with the journey of mastery: it is through commitment to a goal larger than ourselves that we find meaning and fulfillment.

A Call to Embrace Mastery

The rewards of mastery are not confined to a select few — they are available to anyone willing to embrace the discipline of deep work. By dedicating ourselves to focused effort, we unlock the potential for excellence, innovation, and personal growth. Mastery enriches not only our own lives but also the lives of those we touch, creating a ripple effect that extends far beyond individual accomplishments.

As we conclude this chapter, let these rewards serve as a reminder of what is possible when we commit to the journey of mastery. The path may be challenging, but the destination — marked by purpose, fulfillment, and impact — is well worth the effort.

CHAPTER 4: THE COURAGE TO FAIL – LESSONS FROM BOLD INNOVATORS

The Role of Failure in Genius

Failure is often seen as the antithesis of success—a roadblock to be avoided at all costs. Yet, history's greatest innovators have shown us that failure is not the end of the journey but an integral part of the path to greatness. It is through failure that we learn, adapt, and ultimately achieve. From the inventiveness of Thomas Edison to the perseverance of J.K. Rowling and the resilience of Abraham Lincoln, failure has been a powerful teacher, shaping the minds and spirits of those who dared to dream boldly.

Thomas Edison: Failure as a Laboratory for Success

Thomas Edison's legacy is defined by his unparalleled contributions to modern technology, from the phonograph to the electric light bulb. Yet, behind every triumph lay countless failures. Edison famously conducted over 1,000 experiments before successfully inventing a commercially viable light bulb. When asked about his repeated setbacks, Edison responded with characteristic optimism: "I have not failed. I've just found 10,000 ways that won't work."

This perspective reveals a crucial truth about failure: it is not a mark of inadequacy but a process of discovery. For Edison, each failed experiment was a step closer to understanding the principles needed for success. His resilience and unwavering commitment to innovation demonstrate that failure is not something to be feared—it is a necessary companion on the road to mastery.

Edison's story offers a powerful lesson for contemporary readers: failure is a laboratory, not a verdict. When we view setbacks as opportunities to learn and refine our approach, we transform obstacles into stepping stones toward our goals.

J.K. Rowling: From Rejection to Revolution

The world of literature offers its own powerful testament to the role of failure in genius. Before J.K. Rowling became a household name with the *Harry Potter* series, she faced years of rejection and hardship. Struggling as a single mother, Rowling submitted her manuscript to twelve publishers, all of whom rejected it. It wasn't until a small publishing house took a chance on her work that Rowling's life began to change.

Rowling has often spoken about the profound impact of these early failures on her journey. In her Harvard commencement speech, she remarked, "Failure meant a stripping away of the inessential. I stopped pretending to myself that I was anything other than what I was, and began to direct all my energy into finishing the only work that mattered to me." By embracing failure and focusing on her passion, Rowling turned her setbacks into the foundation of a literary empire.

Her story serves as a reminder that failure is not the end of the road but a crucible that refines our vision and determination. For those pursuing their own creative or professional goals, Rowling's journey underscores the importance of resilience and authenticity in the face of adversity.

Abraham Lincoln: Resilience in the Face of Defeat

Perhaps no figure embodies the transformative power of failure more than Abraham Lincoln.

Before becoming the 16th President of the United States and leading the nation through its darkest hours, Lincoln experienced a series of personal and professional defeats. He failed in business, lost multiple elections, and endured profound personal tragedies, including the death of his fiancée and the loss of his young children.

Yet, Lincoln's resilience in the face of these challenges became a defining trait of his leadership. Each failure deepened his empathy, strengthened his resolve, and sharpened his ability to navigate complex political and moral landscapes. When the Civil War threatened to tear the country apart, Lincoln drew upon the lessons of his failures to guide the nation with wisdom and humility.

Lincoln's life offers a profound lesson: failure is not an impediment to greatness—it is often the crucible in which greatness is forged. His story reminds us that the courage to confront setbacks and persist in the face of adversity is the foundation of lasting achievement.

Failure as a Catalyst for Growth

What unites these stories of Edison, Rowling, and Lincoln is not just their extraordinary achievements but their ability to reframe failure as a catalyst for growth. Each of these figures embraced failure as an essential part of their journey, using it to refine their vision, build resilience, and deepen their understanding of their craft. Their experiences remind us that failure is not something to be avoided — it is something to be embraced.

The philosopher Friedrich Nietzsche captured this idea succinctly when he wrote, "That which does not kill us makes us stronger." While failure can be painful and disheartening, it also provides an unparalleled opportunity for growth. By examining our setbacks with curiosity and honesty, we uncover valuable insights that propel us forward.

A New Perspective on Failure

For contemporary readers, the role of failure in genius offers a powerful shift in perspective. Instead of viewing failure as a sign of weakness or inadequacy, we can begin to see it as a necessary step on the path to success. This mindset not only reduces the fear of failure but also empowers us to take bold risks and pursue our goals with greater confidence.

To apply this principle in our own lives, we must cultivate a willingness to experiment and embrace imperfection. Whether launching a new business, pursuing a creative project, or navigating personal challenges, the courage to fail is often the first step toward unlocking our full potential.

A Foundation for Future Success

As we explore the remaining sections of this chapter, we will delve deeper into how to overcome the fear of failure, turn setbacks into stepping stones, and embrace failure as an ongoing process of growth. The stories of Edison, Rowling, and Lincoln remind us that failure is not the opposite of success—it is its foundation. By embracing this truth, we unlock the courage to pursue our boldest dreams and discover the genius within ourselves.

Overcoming Fear of Failure

Failure, though an inevitable part of life, often carries a heavy weight of fear. This fear—of judgment, loss, or the unknown—can stifle creativity, halt risk-taking, and prevent us from pursuing our full potential. Yet, history is rich with stories of individuals who have confronted their fears and emerged stronger, transforming their setbacks into opportunities for growth. By understanding the roots of this fear and employing strategies to overcome it, we can reframe failure as a stepping stone rather than a barrier.

The Weight of Judgment

One of the most paralyzing aspects of failure is the fear of judgment. We live in a world that often equates success with worth, creating a culture where setbacks are seen as personal deficiencies rather than valuable lessons. This fear of judgment is particularly acute in creative and entrepreneurial endeavors, where public scrutiny can feel like an insurmountable obstacle.

Vincent van Gogh's story illustrates the power of perseverance in the face of judgment. During his lifetime, van Gogh sold only one painting, and his work was often dismissed as unrefined or overly emotive. Despite this lack of recognition, he continued to paint prolifically, driven by his passion and belief in his vision. Today, his works are celebrated as masterpieces, a testament to his resilience and refusal to let fear dictate his path.

Van Gogh's journey reminds us that external judgment is often fleeting and subjective. True success lies not in the approval of others but in the courage to stay true to our passions and aspirations. By shifting our focus from external validation to intrinsic motivation, we can free ourselves from the fear of judgment and embrace the creative process.

The Fear of Loss

Another significant barrier to overcoming failure is the fear of loss—whether it be financial security, reputation, or personal relationships. This fear can lead to risk aversion, preventing individuals from pursuing bold ideas or stepping outside their comfort zones. Yet, as many innovators have shown, the greatest rewards often come from taking calculated risks.

Take the example of Elon Musk, whose ambitious ventures into electric vehicles and space exploration were fraught with financial and technical challenges. At one point, Musk faced the possibility of losing both Tesla and SpaceX, risking his entire fortune to keep his dreams alive. Rather than succumbing to fear, he chose to double down on his vision, ultimately achieving groundbreaking success in both industries.

Musk's story highlights the importance of resilience and strategic risk-taking. While the fear of loss is natural, it can be mitigated by careful planning, a clear vision, and a willingness to adapt. For readers, this means embracing the possibility of setbacks while remaining focused on long-term goals. Losses are not the end of the story—they are part of the journey toward growth and innovation.

The Psychological Roots of Fear

To overcome the fear of failure, it is essential to understand its psychological roots. Fear often stems from our brain's natural inclination to prioritize safety and avoid uncertainty. This response, while useful in situations of physical danger, can become counterproductive when applied to creative or professional challenges.

Neuroscientist Dr. Srini Pillay explores this concept in his work, emphasizing the importance of rewiring our mental approach to fear. By recognizing fear as a signal rather than a stop sign, we can learn to navigate it with curiosity and courage. Instead of avoiding situations that provoke fear, we can view them as opportunities to push boundaries and expand our comfort zones.

Mindfulness practices, such as meditation and journaling, can also help in managing fear. By cultivating self-awareness, we can better understand our triggers and develop strategies to address them. This process not only reduces the intensity of fear but also enhances our ability to respond thoughtfully rather than react impulsively.

Strategies for Confronting Fear

Overcoming the fear of failure requires both mindset shifts and practical strategies. One effective approach is to reframe failure as feed-back. Rather than viewing setbacks as person-al shortcomings, we can see them as valuable data points that guide us toward improvement. Thomas Edison exemplified this perspective, famously stating, "I have not failed. I've just found 10,000 ways that won't work." By adopt-ing a similar mindset, we can transform fear into curiosity, approaching challenges with a spirit of exploration.

Another strategy is to start small and build con-fidence through incremental successes. This principle, often referred to as "scaling risk," involves breaking down ambitious goals into manageable steps. Each small achievement not only reduces the fear of failure but also builds momentum, making larger risks feel more at-tainable.

Support networks also play a crucial role in overcoming fear. Surrounding ourselves with mentors, peers, and collaborators who encour-age experimentation and provide constructive feedback can make the process of risk-taking less daunting. These relationships remind us that we are not alone in our struggles and that failure is a shared and universal experience.

Reframing Failure as Growth

One of the most powerful ways to overcome fear is to reframe failure as an integral part of growth. This perspective is deeply rooted in the concept of a growth mindset, popularized by psychologist Carol Dweck. A growth mindset emphasizes the belief that abilities and intelligence can be developed through effort and learning. By embracing this outlook, we can view failure not as a permanent condition but as a stepping stone to improvement.

Historical figures like Abraham Lincoln exemplify this approach. Lincoln's numerous failures in business and politics did not deter him; instead, they strengthened his resolve and deepened his understanding of leadership. His journey reminds us that setbacks are not obstacles to be avoided — they are opportunities to build resilience, learn valuable lessons, and refine our goals.

The Freedom of Letting Go

Ultimately, overcoming the fear of failure requires letting go of the need for certainty and control. As the poet Rainer Maria Rilke wrote, "You must give birth to your images. They are the future waiting to be born. Fear not the strangeness you feel. The future must enter you long before it happens." This willingness to embrace uncertainty is the hallmark of bold innovators and creators.

By accepting that failure is an inevitable part of any meaningful endeavor, we free ourselves to take risks, experiment, and pursue our dreams with authenticity. The path to success is rarely linear, but it is through navigating its twists and turns that we discover our greatest potential.

A Call to Courage

As we explore the remaining sections of this chapter, let the stories and strategies for overcoming fear serve as a guide. Fear of failure, though powerful, is not insurmountable. By confronting it with intention and resilience, we unlock the courage to take bold steps toward our goals. The rewards of this journey are not just professional or creative—they are deeply

personal, enriching our understanding of ourselves and our capacity for growth.

Turning Setbacks into Stepping Stones

Failure, while painful and often humbling, holds the potential to become one of life's most powerful teachers. History abounds with ex-amples of individuals who used their setbacks not as stopping points but as springboards to unparalleled success. By examining these sto-ries, we can uncover the principles and mind-sets that allow failure to be transformed into a foundation for achievement. These lessons remind us that setbacks, though inevitable, are not definitive—they are moments of redirection, discovery, and growth.

Oprah Winfrey: Rejection as Redirection

Before becoming one of the most influential media moguls in history, Oprah Winfrey faced a professional setback that could have derailed her career. Early in her journey, Winfrey was fired from her role as a news anchor in Balti-more, with critics citing her emotional delivery as a liability. What others saw as a weakness, however, Winfrey reframed as a strength. Rather than abandoning her ambitions, she leaned into her authentic voice and shifted her focus toward talk shows, a format that allowed her empathetic and conversational style to shine.

This redirection led to the creation of *The Oprah Winfrey Show*, a groundbreaking program that redefined daytime television and established her as a cultural icon. Reflecting on her journey, Winfrey has often credited her firing as a pivotal moment that forced her to align her work with her true talents and passions. Her story illustrates a powerful truth: setbacks often reveal opportunities that were previously hidden, guiding us toward paths better suited to our strengths.

For readers, the lesson is clear: rejection is not an endpoint—it is a form of redirection. By viewing setbacks as opportunities to reassess and realign, we can uncover new avenues for growth and success.

Steve Jobs: Failure as Reinvention

Few stories of turning setbacks into stepping stones are as dramatic as that of Steve Jobs. In 1985, Jobs was ousted from Apple, the company he co-founded, after a power struggle with the board of directors. This public and deeply personal failure could have marked the end of his career. Instead, Jobs used the experience as an opportunity for reinvention.

In the years following his departure from Apple, Jobs founded NeXT, a company that developed advanced computing technology, and acquired Pixar, a small animation studio with enormous potential. These ventures not only showcased his resilience but also laid the groundwork for his eventual return to Apple in 1997. Armed with new insights and experiences, Jobs led Apple to unprecedented success, introducing products like the iPhone and iPad that revolutionized technology and design.

Jobs often described his ousting from Apple as one of the most liberating periods of his life, freeing him to explore new ideas and approaches. His journey highlights a key principle: failure is not a dead end — it is an invitation to innovate, evolve, and return stronger than before.

Malala Yousafzai: Adversity as a Platform for Change

Not all setbacks stem from professional challenges; some arise from profound personal adversity. Malala Yousafzai's story is a testament to the human spirit's capacity to transform even the most harrowing experiences into a platform for change. In 2012, Malala was targeted and shot by the Taliban for advocating for girls' education in Pakistan. Rather than silencing her, this violent attack galvanized her mission and brought global attention to her cause.

Recovering from her injuries, Malala became an international advocate for education and women's rights, co-founding the Malala Fund and becoming the youngest-ever recipient of the Nobel Peace Prize. Her resilience and determination turned a personal tragedy into a catalyst for global impact, inspiring millions to join her fight for equality.

Malala's story underscores the transformative power of purpose. When setbacks are viewed through the lens of a higher mission, they become fuel for action, enabling us to turn pain into progress and challenges into catalysts for change.

Walt Disney: Persistence Amid Repeated Failures

Walt Disney's name is synonymous with creativity and innovation, but his journey to success was far from smooth. Before building his entertainment empire, Disney faced numerous failures, including the bankruptcy of his first animation studio and the loss of key characters to competitors. Yet, these setbacks did not deter him. Instead, Disney continued to innovate, eventually creating Mickey Mouse and launching *Snow White and the Seven Dwarfs*, the first full-length animated feature film.

Disney's ability to persevere through failure was rooted in his unwavering belief in his vision. He once remarked, "All the adversity I've had in my life, all my troubles and obstacles, have strengthened me. You may not realize it when it happens, but a kick in the teeth may be the best thing in the world for you." His story demonstrates that persistence, even in the face of repeated setbacks, is often the key to achieving extraordinary success.

For those navigating their own challenges, Disney's journey serves as a reminder that resilience and creativity go hand in hand. Setbacks are not roadblocks—they are opportunities to innovate and redefine what is possible.

Turning Setbacks Into Stepping Stones

The common thread in these stories is not the absence of failure but the willingness to confront it, learn from it, and use it as a stepping stone to greater heights. Each of these individuals faced moments of doubt, pain, and uncertainty, yet they emerged stronger, more focused, and more determined.

The process of turning setbacks into stepping stones begins with a mindset shift. Rather than viewing failure as a reflection of personal inadequacy, we must see it as a natural and necessary part of growth. This perspective allows us to approach challenges with curiosity and resilience, transforming obstacles into opportunities for learning and innovation.

Practical Applications for Readers

To apply these lessons in our own lives, we can start by reframing failure as feedback. Each setback provides valuable information about what works, what doesn't, and where adjustments are needed. By analyzing our failures with honesty and objectivity, we can uncover insights that propel us forward.

Another key practice is cultivating patience and persistence. As the stories of Winfrey, Jobs, Malala, and Disney illustrate, success often requires enduring multiple setbacks before achieving a breakthrough. By maintaining a long-term perspective and staying committed to our goals, we can navigate the inevitable ups and downs of the journey.

Finally, it is essential to embrace adaptability. Setbacks often force us to reconsider our strategies and explore alternative paths. This flexibility not only helps us overcome challenges but also opens doors to opportunities we may not have otherwise considered.

A New Perspective on Failure

The ability to turn setbacks into stepping stones is not a rare talent—it is a skill that can be cultivated through practice, resilience, and a willingness to learn. As we continue to explore the themes of this chapter, let these stories serve as a source of inspiration and guidance. Failure is not an end—it is a beginning, a chance to reinvent ourselves and pursue our dreams with renewed purpose and determination.

Embracing Failure as a Process

Failure, when viewed through the right lens, ceases to be a burden and transforms into a teacher. It is not a singular event to be feared but a recurring process inherent to growth and achievement. From artists to scientists, and from entrepreneurs to athletes, those who achieve greatness understand that failure is not just a possibility—it is a necessity. Embracing failure as a process allows us to unlock our potential, refine our goals, and discover new paths forward.

Failure as a Feedback Loop

One of the most powerful ways to reframe failure is to view it as a feedback loop. In this perspective, each setback provides valuable information about what works and what doesn't. This iterative process is particularly evident in the world of innovation, where trial and error often drive progress.

Consider the journey of James Dyson, the inventor of the Dyson vacuum cleaner. Dyson spent 15 years and created 5,127 prototypes before arriving at the final design. Each failed prototype was not a defeat but a source of data, guiding him closer to his goal. His persistence paid off, leading to the creation of a globally successful product and redefining the standards of household technology.

For readers, Dyson's story offers a simple yet profound insight: failure is not the opposite of success—it is the scaffolding upon which success is built. By treating failure as a source of feedback rather than a personal indictment, we can cultivate a mindset that embraces experimentation and continuous improvement.

The Philosophy of Incremental Growth

The Japanese concept of *kaizen*, or continuous improvement, exemplifies the idea of embracing failure as a process. Rooted in the belief that small, consistent changes lead to significant progress over time, *kaizen* encourages individuals to view setbacks as opportunities to refine their approach. This philosophy has been widely adopted in industries ranging from manufacturing to personal development, offering a blueprint for growth that is both sustainable and resilient.

An illustrative example of *kaizen* can be found in the story of Toyota, a company that revolutionized the automotive industry through its commitment to incremental improvement. When errors occurred on the production line, they were not seen as failures to be hidden but as opportunities to learn and innovate. This mindset allowed Toyota to create a culture of excellence, where every challenge contributed to the company's long-term success.

For individuals, adopting a *kaizen* mindset means embracing the small wins and lessons that come from each attempt. It shifts the focus

from perfection to progress, fostering resilience
and encouraging sustained effort over time.

Failure as a Tool for Self-Discovery

Beyond its practical benefits, failure also serves
as a powerful tool for self-discovery. When we
encounter setbacks, we are forced to confront
our assumptions, reassess our priorities, and
deepen our understanding of ourselves. This
process, while uncomfortable, often leads to
profound personal growth.

The story of Nelson Mandela exemplifies this
principle. Imprisoned for 27 years, Mandela
faced countless challenges and failures in his
fight against apartheid. Yet, during his time in
captivity, he used the experience to reflect on
his values, refine his strategies, and strengthen
his resolve. When he emerged from prison, he
did so not with bitterness but with a vision for
reconciliation and unity, becoming one of history's most transformative leaders.

Mandela's journey reminds us that failure is
not merely an external event—it is an internal
process that shapes who we are. By embracing

the introspection that failure demands, we can uncover our true strengths and chart a path forward with clarity and purpose.

The Role of Community in Embracing Failure

While failure is often experienced as a solitary struggle, it does not have to be faced alone. Communities and support networks play a vital role in helping individuals navigate setbacks and find meaning in their experiences. By sharing our failures with others, we not only reduce the stigma surrounding them but also gain valuable insights and encouragement.

The tech industry offers a compelling example of this dynamic. Events like FailCon, a conference dedicated to exploring the lessons learned from failure, provide a platform for entrepreneurs to share their stories and support one another. These gatherings foster a culture of transparency and collaboration, demonstrating that failure is a shared and essential part of innovation.

For readers, the takeaway is clear: surrounding ourselves with supportive and like-minded individuals can make the process of embracing failure more manageable and rewarding. Whether through mentorship, peer groups, or professional networks, these connections remind us that failure is not a solitary burden — it is a collective experience that unites us all.

Reframing Failure as Growth

At its core, embracing failure as a process requires a fundamental shift in perspective. Rather than viewing setbacks as obstacles to be avoided, we must see them as stepping stones on the path to growth. This mindset shift not only reduces the fear of failure but also empowers us to take risks and pursue our goals with greater confidence.

Philosopher John Dewey captured this sentiment when he wrote, "Failure is instructive. The person who really thinks learns quite as much from his failures as from his successes." Dewey's words highlight an essential truth: failure is not an endpoint but a bridge, connecting us to deeper understanding and greater achievement.

For readers, adopting this mindset means asking reflective questions in the face of setbacks:

What can I learn from this experience? How can I apply these lessons moving forward? By approaching failure with curiosity and openness, we transform it from a source of frustration into a catalyst for growth.

Practical Steps to Embrace Failure

While the philosophy of embracing failure is inspiring, its application requires deliberate action. One practical step is to cultivate a habit of reflection, using tools like journaling to document and analyze setbacks. This practice not only clarifies the lessons learned but also helps to identify patterns and opportunities for improvement.

Another approach is to reframe failure through storytelling. Sharing our experiences with others, whether in a personal or professional setting, allows us to process and normalize failure. These narratives become a source of empowerment, reminding us that failure is a universal experience and a vital part of the human journey.

Finally, it is essential to celebrate effort, not just outcomes. By valuing the courage it takes to try—regardless of the result—we create a culture that encourages experimentation and resilience. This shift in focus allows us to embrace failure as a natural and valuable part of the creative process.

A Call to Embrace the Journey

As we conclude this chapter, let the lessons of failure serve as a beacon of hope and possibility. Failure, though often feared, is one of life's greatest teachers, offering us the chance to learn, grow, and discover our true potential. By embracing failure as a process, we unlock the courage to take bold steps toward our goals, knowing that each setback brings us closer to success.

The journey of failure is not easy, but it is transformative. As we face the challenges and uncertainties of life, may we do so with the resilience, curiosity, and determination that define the bold innovators who came before us. Failure is not the end—it is the beginning of something extraordinary.

CHAPTER 5: THE POWER OF COLLABORATION – GENIUS IN TEAMWORK

Historical Collaborations That Changed the World

The myth of the solitary genius—an individual toiling away in isolation to create groundbreaking work—has long dominated cultural narratives. Yet, history tells a different story. Some of humanity's most transformative achievements were not the result of singular efforts but of collaboration: the coming together of diverse talents, perspectives, and skills to accomplish something extraordinary. From the harmonious melodies of The Beatles to the scientific breakthroughs of the Manhattan Project, these stories demonstrate that collective effort can amplify genius, unlocking possibilities that no individual could achieve alone.

The Beatles: Harmony in Diversity

When John Lennon, Paul McCartney, George Harrison, and Ringo Starr came together to form The Beatles, they created more than just a band—they ignited a cultural revolution. Each member brought unique strengths to the group: Lennon's introspective lyricism, McCartney's melodic inventiveness, Harrison's soulful guitar work, and Starr's rhythmic precision. Together, their collaborative synergy produced a body of work that not only defined an era but continues to inspire musicians and listeners worldwide.

The Beatles' success was not merely a product of individual talent; it was the result of their ability to balance creative tension with mutual respect. Their songwriting partnership, particularly between Lennon and McCartney, exemplified the power of collaboration. While their approaches often differed—Lennon favoring raw emotion and McCartney leaning toward polished composition—their combined efforts created songs that were greater than the sum of their parts.

The lesson for modern readers is clear: collaboration thrives when individuals bring their unique gifts to the table while embracing the strengths of others. By finding harmony in diversity, we can create work that transcends individual limitations and resonates on a universal scale.

The Manhattan Project: A Collective Quest for Innovation

While The Beatles exemplify creative collaboration, the Manhattan Project illustrates the power of teamwork in scientific and technological innovation. During World War II, some of the world's brightest minds, including J. Robert Oppenheimer, Enrico Fermi, and Richard Feynman, came together to develop the first atomic bomb. Their mission, though fraught with ethical complexities, required an unprecedented level of collaboration across disciplines and institutions.

The Manhattan Project succeeded not only because of the intellectual brilliance of its contributors but also because of their ability to coordinate efforts and share knowledge. Physicists, chemists, engineers, and military personnel worked in tandem, overcoming technical and logistical challenges that had never been faced before. Their collective ingenuity not only ended the war but also ushered in a new era of scientific discovery.

This example underscores the importance of trust and communication in collaborative endeavors. The Manhattan Project was built on a foundation of shared purpose, with each participant understanding the critical role they played in the larger mission. For readers seeking to enhance their own teamwork skills, the takeaway is profound: effective collaboration requires both individual excellence and a commitment to the collective goal.

The Apollo Program: Reaching for the Stars Together

Another powerful testament to the transformative potential of collaboration is NASA's Apollo program, which achieved the historic moon landing in 1969. The program brought together more than 400,000 people, including scientists, engineers, astronauts, and support staff, all working toward the audacious goal of sending humans to the moon and bringing them safely back to Earth.

The success of Apollo 11 was the result of meticulous planning, rigorous testing, and, above all, an unwavering belief in the power of teamwork. Astronaut Neil Armstrong may have taken the first step on the lunar surface, but his achievement was made possible by countless others, from Katherine Johnson's groundbreaking calculations to the engineers who designed the spacecraft.

The Apollo program reminds us that collaboration often requires humility and a willingness to rely on the expertise of others. By embracing a shared vision and supporting one another's contributions, we can accomplish feats that once seemed impossible.

The Value of Collective Wisdom

These historical examples highlight a fundamental truth about collaboration: it leverages collective wisdom. When diverse perspectives come together, they create a rich tapestry of ideas, insights, and solutions. This principle is not limited to grand achievements; it applies to everyday challenges, from solving workplace problems to fostering innovation in communities.

The 20th-century psychologist Lev Vygotsky explored this concept in his work on social learning theory, emphasizing that human development occurs through interaction and collaboration. His insights resonate with modern organizational practices, where teamwork and knowledge sharing are recognized as drivers of success. For readers, the implication is clear: seeking out diverse viewpoints and engaging in collaborative dialogue can unlock new levels of creativity and understanding.

Lessons for the Present and Future

The stories of The Beatles, the Manhattan Project, and the Apollo program demonstrate that collaboration is not just a tool for achieving great things—it is a mindset that values connection, trust, and shared purpose. In today's increasingly interconnected world, these principles are more relevant than ever. Technology and globalization have created opportunities for collaboration on a scale previously unimaginable, allowing individuals and organizations to pool their talents and resources to address complex global challenges.

As we move forward, the lessons of history remind us that true collaboration is not about suppressing individuality but about amplifying it within the context of a larger goal. By embracing the power of teamwork, we can create solutions that honor the contributions of every participant while achieving outcomes that benefit all.

A Call to Collaborate

The power of collaboration lies in its ability to unite diverse talents, perspectives, and passions toward a common purpose. As we reflect on these historical examples, let them inspire us to seek out opportunities for connection and cooperation in our own lives. Whether we are creating art, advancing science, or building communities, the lessons of The Beatles, the Manhattan Project, and the Apollo program remind us that together, we are capable of greatness.

Balancing Independence and Teamwork

The tension between independence and teamwork is a paradox at the heart of collaboration. On one hand, individuals bring unique strengths, ideas, and perspectives that fuel innovation and creativity. On the other hand, the power of collaboration lies in harmonizing these diverse contributions to achieve a shared goal. The art of balancing independence and teamwork requires not only self-awareness but also an understanding of how to integrate individual efforts into a cohesive whole.

The Symphony of Individuality in Collaboration

A compelling metaphor for balancing independence and teamwork can be found in the world of music, particularly in orchestras. Each musician in an orchestra is a master of their instrument, capable of delivering a solo performance. Yet, when they come together under the direction of a conductor, their collective effort produces something far greater than the sum of its parts. The violinist's precision, the cellist's depth, and the percussionist's rhythm combine to create a symphony that resonates with audiences on a profound level.

This interplay between individual excellence and collective harmony reflects the dynamics of effective teamwork. Just as each musician must maintain their unique voice while aligning with the group's vision, individuals in collaborative environments must strike a balance between asserting their ideas and contributing to the team's objectives. This balance requires both confidence in one's abilities and a willingness to adapt and support others.

Historical Examples of Balanced Collaboration

One of the most striking examples of balancing independence and teamwork comes from the Wright brothers, Orville and Wilbur, whose partnership led to the invention of the airplane. While their collaboration was deeply inter-twined, each brother brought distinct skills to the endeavor. Orville excelled in mechanics and experimentation, while Wilbur was a me-ticulous planner and strategist. Their ability to respect and leverage each other's strengths allowed them to achieve what many thought impossible.

Similarly, the collaborative relationship be-tween choreographer Jerome Robbins and composer Leonard Bernstein, who worked to-gether on *West Side Story*, exemplifies the power of balancing individual genius within a team. Robbins's vision for the dance and movement of the production complemented Bernstein's dynamic musical composition, resulting in a groundbreaking work that redefined musical theater. Their mutual respect and open communication ensured that each of their contributions enhanced the other's work.

These stories remind us that effective collaboration does not require individuals to suppress their unique talents. Instead, it thrives when those talents are celebrated and integrated into a larger vision.

The Importance of Clear Roles and Boundaries

One of the keys to balancing independence and teamwork is establishing clear roles and boundaries within a group. When individuals understand their responsibilities and how their work contributes to the team's goals, they can focus on their strengths without feeling the need to micromanage or compete with others. This clarity fosters trust and allows each team member to operate with autonomy while staying aligned with the collective mission.

Consider the example of a film production crew. The director, cinematographer, screenwriter, and actors each play distinct roles, yet their efforts must converge to create a cohesive film. The director may guide the overall vision, but they rely on the expertise of others to bring that vision to life. When roles are clearly defined, each contributor can take ownership of their work, knowing that their efforts are valued and supported.

For readers, the lesson is clear: defining roles and expectations within a team creates the foundation for both individual and collective success. By clarifying how each person's contribution fits into the bigger picture, we empower individuals to excel while fostering a sense of unity.

Navigating Creative Tension

While collaboration often involves harmony, it can also generate creative tension—a dynamic that, when managed effectively, can lead to breakthroughs. Creative tension arises when differing perspectives and ideas clash, forcing individuals to question assumptions and explore new possibilities. This tension, though uncomfortable, is an essential driver of innovation.

The relationship between Steve Jobs and Apple designer Jony Ive illustrates this principle. Jobs's relentless pursuit of perfection often collided with Ive's creative process, leading to intense discussions and debates. However, this tension ultimately resulted in groundbreaking designs, from the iPhone to the MacBook, that redefined technology and aesthetics.

To navigate creative tension, it is crucial to foster an environment of psychological safety, where team members feel comfortable expressing dissenting opinions without fear of judgment or retaliation. By embracing constructive conflict and encouraging open dialogue, teams can transform tension into a catalyst for growth and innovation.

The Role of Self-Awareness in Collaboration

Balancing independence and teamwork also requires self-awareness. Individuals must understand their strengths, weaknesses, and working styles to contribute effectively to a team. This self-awareness enables them to recognize when to assert their ideas and when to step back and support others.

A practical approach to developing self-awareness in collaboration is the use of personality

assessments and feedback tools, such as the
Myers-Briggs Type Indicator or StrengthsFind-
er. These tools help individuals identify their
natural tendencies and how they interact with
others, fostering greater empathy and collaboration.

For example, an extroverted team member may
excel at generating ideas in brainstorming sessions but may need to practice active listening
during discussions. Conversely, an introverted
member might shine in focused problem-solving tasks but may benefit from finding ways
to share their insights more openly. By understanding these dynamics, individuals can adapt
their approach to better align with the needs of
the team.

Celebrating Individuality Within the Collec-
tive

Ultimately, the most effective teams are those
that celebrate individuality while working toward a shared purpose. This principle is evident
in the natural world, where ecosystems thrive
through diversity. Each species in an ecosystem
plays a unique role, contributing to the bal-

ance and health of the whole. Similarly, human collaboration flourishes when individuals are encouraged to bring their full selves to the table, enriching the collective with their diverse perspectives and talents.

For readers, this means embracing both their individuality and their interconnectedness. By valuing their own contributions while recognizing the importance of others' input, they can strike the delicate balance that makes collaboration not only productive but also deeply fulfilling.

A Call to Balance

Balancing independence and teamwork is not about compromising one's identity or ideas—it is about finding harmony in diversity. As the stories of the Wright brothers, Jerome Robbins, and others illustrate, collaboration thrives when individuals bring their unique strengths to the collective effort. By embracing clear roles, navigating creative tension, and fostering self-awareness, we can create environments where both individuality and teamwork flourish.

As we explore the next sections of this chapter, let these principles serve as a foundation for understanding how to build effective partnerships and adapt to the evolving dynamics of collaboration in the modern world. Together, we can achieve more than we ever could alone.

Building Effective Partnerships

Effective partnerships are the backbone of successful collaborations. They thrive on trust, communication, and mutual respect—qualities that transform disparate individuals into cohesive teams. While the journey to building such partnerships can be challenging, it is also deeply rewarding. By understanding the dynamics of effective teamwork and employing strategies to foster these qualities, we can create relationships that not only achieve great things but also enrich the lives of those involved.

Trust: The Foundation of Collaboration

At the heart of every effective partnership lies trust. Without it, even the most talented teams can falter, as doubt and suspicion undermine their ability to work together. Trust enables individuals to take risks, share ideas, and rely on one another, creating a sense of psychological safety that is essential for innovation.

A powerful example of trust in action can be seen in the collaboration between Anne Sullivan and Helen Keller. When Sullivan first began working with Keller, a young girl who was deaf and blind, their relationship was fraught with challenges. Keller's frustration and inability to communicate created significant barriers. Yet, through patience, persistence, and unwavering belief in Keller's potential, Sullivan built a foundation of trust. This bond allowed Keller to embrace learning and eventually achieve extraordinary success as a writer and advocate.

Sullivan and Keller's story underscores the transformative power of trust. For readers, building trust in partnerships begins with

being reliable and consistent in actions and communication. Honoring commitments, demonstrating integrity, and showing empathy are the cornerstones of cultivating trust. By fostering a safe environment where team members feel valued and supported, we lay the groundwork for meaningful collaboration.

Communication: The Lifeblood of Partnerships

While trust establishes the foundation, effective communication serves as the lifeblood of partnerships. Open and transparent dialogue ensures that team members remain aligned, misunderstandings are minimized, and ideas can flow freely. Communication is not merely about speaking—it is about listening, understanding, and responding in ways that advance the shared goal.

One striking example of the power of communication is the teamwork behind the Apollo 13 mission. When an explosion jeopardized the lives of three astronauts in space, it was the clear and constant communication between the crew and mission control that brought them safely back to Earth. Engineers, scientists, and astronauts collaborated in real time, exchanging critical information and problem-solving under immense pressure. Their ability to communicate effectively underlined the importance of clarity, precision, and mutual respect in high-stakes situations.

For readers, mastering communication in partnerships involves not only articulating thoughts clearly but also practicing active listening. By giving others the space to express their perspectives, we create an environment where all voices are heard, and the collective intelligence of the team can emerge.

Mutual Respect: Embracing Diversity and Equality

Mutual respect is the glue that holds partnerships together, especially in diverse teams where individuals bring varying skills, experiences, and viewpoints. Respecting each team member's contributions fosters a culture of inclusion and collaboration, where differences are seen as assets rather than obstacles.

The partnership between Pixar co-founder Ed Catmull and director John Lasseter exemplifies mutual respect in action. Catmull, a computer scientist, and Lasseter, an animator, came from different disciplines, yet their collaboration revolutionized the animation industry. By valuing each other's expertise and working as equals, they created groundbreaking films like *Toy Story*, which blended technology and storytelling in unprecedented ways.

This example highlights a critical lesson: effective partnerships thrive when individuals recognize and appreciate the strengths of others. For readers, cultivating mutual respect requires acknowledging the value of diverse perspectives and creating an environment where everyone feels empowered to contribute.

Navigating Conflict with Grace

No partnership is without conflict. However, how conflicts are handled often determines the success of a collaboration. Productive conflict resolution involves addressing disagreements constructively, focusing on the issue rather than the person, and finding solutions that benefit the team as a whole.

The dynamic between Mahatma Gandhi and Jawaharlal Nehru during India's struggle for independence illustrates this principle. While Gandhi and Nehru shared the same overarching vision, their approaches often diverged, leading to disagreements. Yet, they resolved their conflicts with mutual respect and a commitment to their shared mission, enabling them to lead India toward independence.

For readers, learning to navigate conflict with grace involves approaching disagreements with curiosity and empathy. By seeking to understand the underlying concerns and working collaboratively to address them, we can transform conflict into an opportunity for growth and innovation.

Practical Strategies for Building Effective Partnerships

Creating partnerships rooted in trust, communication, and respect requires intentional effort. One practical strategy is to establish clear expectations and goals at the outset of a collaboration. This clarity helps align individual efforts with the team's objectives and minimizes misunderstandings.

Regular check-ins and feedback sessions are another valuable tool. These interactions provide opportunities to address concerns, celebrate progress, and adjust strategies as needed. By fostering a culture of continuous improvement, teams can maintain momentum and adapt to changing circumstances.

Another powerful approach is to celebrate successes together. Acknowledging the contributions of each team member and sharing in the joy of achievements strengthens bonds and reinforces the value of collaboration.

The Ripple Effect of Effective Partnerships

The benefits of building effective partnerships extend beyond the immediate task at hand. When individuals experience the power of trust, communication, and respect in a team setting, they carry those principles into other areas of their lives. Strong partnerships inspire confidence, deepen connections, and create a sense of belonging that enhances both personal and professional growth.

The ripple effect of effective collaboration is evident in the stories of great partnerships throughout history. From the creative synergy of The Beatles to the scientific breakthroughs of the Manhattan Project, these examples remind us that when people come together with purpose and mutual respect, their potential is limitless.

A Call to Build Together

As we reflect on the qualities that make partnerships thrive, let us embrace the challenge of building connections that amplify our strengths and broaden our horizons. Trust, communication, and respect are not just abstract ideals — they are practices that, when nurtured, unlock the full potential of collaboration.

As we explore the final section of this chapter, we will turn our gaze to the future of teamwork, examining how technology and globalization are reshaping the way we collaborate. But the principles of effective partnerships remain timeless, reminding us that at the heart of every great achievement is the power of working together.

The Future of Collaboration

Collaboration has always been a cornerstone

of human achievement, but the way we work together is undergoing a profound transformation. As technology continues to evolve and globalization knits the world closer together, new paradigms of teamwork are emerging. These changes present both opportunities and challenges, requiring us to adapt and rethink how we connect, create, and innovate. By understanding the trends shaping the future of collaboration, we can position ourselves to thrive in an increasingly interconnected world.

Technology as a Catalyst for Global Collaboration

The digital revolution has redefined the boundaries of teamwork, enabling people to collaborate across vast distances in real time. Tools like video conferencing, cloud storage, and collaborative software have not only increased efficiency but also expanded the scope of what is possible. Teams can now bring together experts from around the globe, leveraging diverse perspectives and expertise to solve complex problems.

One powerful example of this phenomenon is

the open-source software movement. Projects like Linux and Wikipedia exemplify how distributed collaboration can produce extraordinary results. These initiatives thrive on the contributions of individuals from all walks of life, united by a shared vision and enabled by digital platforms. Contributors often work asynchronously, communicating through online forums and sharing updates in real time, demonstrating the potential of technology to amplify collective intelligence.

For readers, the lesson is clear: the ability to harness technology effectively is no longer optional—it is a critical skill for participating in the future of collaboration. By mastering digital tools and embracing virtual teamwork, we can unlock new opportunities to contribute and innovate on a global scale.

The Rise of Remote and Hybrid Work

The COVID-19 pandemic accelerated the shift toward remote and hybrid work, fundamentally altering the dynamics of collaboration. While the transition posed challenges, it also highlighted the potential for flexibility and inclusivity in the workplace. Remote work has allowed companies to tap into talent pools previously inaccessible due to geographic constraints, fostering greater diversity and innovation.

However, the remote work revolution has also underscored the importance of intentional communication and relationship-building. Without the organic interactions of a shared physical space, teams must find new ways to foster connection and trust. Virtual team-building activities, regular check-ins, and clear communication channels have become essential for maintaining cohesion and morale.

As hybrid work models continue to evolve, the key will be striking a balance between flexibility and structure. For individuals and organizations alike, this means embracing adaptability and prioritizing human connection, even in virtual environments.

Globalization and Cross-Cultural Collaboration

Globalization has brought people from different cultures, languages, and perspectives into closer contact than ever before. While this diversity enriches collaboration, it also requires a heightened awareness of cultural dynamics and communication styles. Effective cross-cultural collaboration depends on mutual respect, openness, and a willingness to navigate differences.

The success of the Human Genome Project, an international research effort to map the human genome, illustrates the power of global collaboration. Scientists from multiple countries worked together over more than a decade, sharing data and insights to achieve a groundbreaking scientific milestone. Their ability to transcend national and cultural boundaries exemplifies the potential of global teamwork to tackle complex challenges.

For readers, the takeaway is that cultural competence is an increasingly valuable skill. By developing an understanding of different traditions, values, and communication norms, we can build stronger relationships and contribute more effectively to diverse teams.

The Role of Artificial Intelligence in Collaboration

Artificial intelligence (AI) is poised to play a transformative role in the future of collaboration. From automating repetitive tasks to generating insights from vast datasets, AI has the potential to enhance productivity and creativity in unprecedented ways. Tools like natural language processing, predictive analytics, and generative AI are already reshaping how teams work, enabling faster decision-making and more personalized solutions.

However, the integration of AI into collaborative processes also raises important ethical and practical questions. How do we ensure that AI tools are used responsibly and inclusively? What role should human intuition and judgment play in a world increasingly influenced by algorithms? These questions highlight the need for thoughtful engagement with technology, ensuring that AI serves as a complement to human collaboration rather than a replacement.

For individuals and teams, leveraging AI effectively requires both technical literacy and ethical awareness. By staying informed about emerging technologies and considering their implications, we can harness the benefits of AI while preserving the values that make collaboration meaningful.

Sustainability and the Collaborative Imperative

The challenges of the 21st century, from climate change to global health crises, demand unprecedented levels of collaboration. Addressing these complex issues requires not only technological innovation but also a commitment to shared responsibility and collective action. The rise of collaborative initiatives like the United Nations' Sustainable Development Goals (SDGs) demonstrates the power of partnerships to drive progress on a global scale.

For example, the Paris Agreement on climate change represents a landmark in international collaboration, bringing together countries, businesses, and communities to address one of humanity's greatest challenges. While the path forward is fraught with difficulties, the agreement underscores the necessity of working together to create a sustainable future.

For readers, the call to action is clear: collaboration is not just a tool for professional success—it is a moral imperative. By contributing to initiatives that prioritize sustainability and equity, we can help build a world where collaboration serves the greater good.

Preparing for the Future

As we look ahead, the future of collaboration will be shaped by our ability to adapt to new technologies, embrace diversity, and foster meaningful connections. While the tools and contexts may change, the principles that underpin effective teamwork—trust, communication, and mutual respect—will remain constant.

For individuals, preparing for this future means cultivating a growth mindset and staying open to learning. Whether by mastering new technologies, seeking out cross-cultural experiences, or developing emotional intelligence, we can position ourselves to thrive in an ever-evolving landscape of collaboration.

A Vision for Tomorrow

The future of collaboration is bright, filled with

possibilities for innovation, connection, and shared achievement. As technology and globalization continue to reshape the way we work, we have an opportunity to harness these forces for the betterment of humanity. By embracing the principles of effective teamwork and staying attuned to emerging trends, we can create partnerships that not only achieve great things but also leave a lasting legacy.

Let the future of collaboration inspire us to dream boldly, connect deeply, and work together toward a world where collective genius knows no bounds.

CHAPTER 6: THE ROLE OF CURIOSITY – A LIFELONG QUEST FOR KNOWLEDGE

Curiosity as the Engine of Discovery

Curiosity is the spark that ignites the flame of discovery. It is the force that compels us to ask why, to seek answers, and to challenge the status quo. Throughout history, curiosity has driven humanity to uncover the mysteries of the natural world, expand the boundaries of knowledge, and transform ideas into groundbreaking innovations. From Galileo's revolutionary observations to Darwin's theory of evolution and Feynman's explorations into the quantum realm, curiosity has been the wellspring of intellectual and creative progress.

Galileo: A Telescope to the Heavens

In the early 17th century, curiosity drove Galileo Galilei to look beyond the familiar and explore the heavens. Armed with a telescope of his own design, Galileo observed celestial phenomena that contradicted the prevailing belief in an Earth-centered universe. He discovered moons orbiting Jupiter, the phases of Venus, and the rugged surface of the Moon—findings that challenged the geocentric model endorsed by the Catholic Church and supported the heliocentric theory proposed by Copernicus.

Galileo's curiosity did not merely lead to new scientific insights; it sparked a revolution in how humanity understood its place in the cosmos. His willingness to question established doctrines and pursue empirical evidence exemplifies the power of curiosity to drive progress. Galileo's story reminds us that curiosity is not a passive trait—it is an active pursuit, requiring courage, persistence, and a willingness to face resistance.

For modern readers, Galileo's legacy underscores the importance of looking beyond conventional wisdom and exploring uncharted territories. By remaining open to new perspectives and asking bold questions, we too can uncover truths that reshape our understanding of the world.

Darwin: The Wonder of Life's Diversity

Two centuries after Galileo, curiosity guided Charles Darwin on a voyage that would redefine biology. In 1831, Darwin embarked on the HMS Beagle, a journey that took him to the

Galápagos Islands and beyond. Observing the remarkable diversity of life on Earth, Darwin began to ask questions about the origins and adaptations of species.

These questions eventually culminated in his groundbreaking work, *On the Origin of Species*. Darwin's theory of natural selection, which explained how species evolve over time through the survival of advantageous traits, transformed biology and provided a unifying framework for understanding the natural world. His curiosity about the intricate patterns of life led to a profound shift in scientific thought, influencing fields as diverse as genetics, ecology, and anthropology.

Darwin's story highlights the importance of observation and wonder in the pursuit of knowledge. By paying attention to the details of the world around us and following our curiosity wherever it leads, we open ourselves to discoveries that have the power to transform our understanding of life itself.

Feynman: Curiosity in the Quantum Realm

If Galileo explored the cosmos and Darwin unraveled the mysteries of life, Richard Feynman delved into the subatomic world, revealing the complexities of quantum mechanics. A Nobel Prize-winning physicist, Feynman was renowned not only for his intellectual brilliance but also for his insatiable curiosity.

Feynman's approach to science was playful and exploratory. He often described his work as "finding out the way things work," whether it involved understanding the behavior of electrons or investigating the mechanics of a spinning plate. His curiosity extended beyond physics; he explored art, music, and even deciphered Mayan hieroglyphs. For Feynman, curiosity was a way of life—a mindset that transcended disciplines and enriched every aspect of his existence.

One of Feynman's most celebrated contributions, the development of Feynman diagrams, simplified complex quantum interactions into intuitive visual representations. These diagrams not only advanced theoretical physics but also demonstrated how curiosity can lead to innovative ways of thinking and problem-solving.

Feynman's story reminds us that curiosity is not confined to academic or professional pursuits — it is a fundamental aspect of being human. By nurturing our innate desire to explore, we cultivate a mindset that embraces complexity, creativity, and joy.

The Philosophical Roots of Curiosity

Curiosity has long been celebrated by philosophers as a cornerstone of intellectual growth. Aristotle described humans as "by nature creatures who desire to know," emphasizing that curiosity is an essential aspect of our being. Similarly, Socrates, the father of Western philosophy, championed the practice of questioning as a means of uncovering truth and cultivating wisdom.

In the modern era, philosophers like Albert Einstein and Carl Sagan have echoed these sentiments, advocating for curiosity as a driver of discovery and wonder. Einstein famously remarked, "I have no special talent. I am only passionately curious," while Sagan wrote about the "exquisite interweaving of curiosity, discovery, and the sheer delight of understanding."

These reflections remind us that curiosity is not merely an intellectual exercise—it is a deeply human trait that connects us to the mysteries of existence. By embracing curiosity, we tap into a wellspring of creativity, resilience, and fulfillment.

Practical Lessons from History's Curious Minds

The stories of Galileo, Darwin, and Feynman offer timeless lessons for cultivating curiosity in our own lives. First, they remind us of the importance of asking questions. Whether questioning established beliefs, as Galileo did, or exploring the details of nature, like Darwin, curiosity begins with the courage to wonder.

Second, these thinkers demonstrate the value of perseverance. Curiosity is not always met with immediate rewards; it often involves setbacks, challenges, and resistance. Yet, as these stories show, the pursuit of knowledge is worth the effort.

Finally, they highlight the power of interdisciplinary exploration. Feynman's curiosity extended beyond physics to art and culture, enriching his life and work. By pursuing diverse interests and embracing curiosity in all its forms, we can expand our horizons and uncover unexpected connections.

A Call to Curiosity

As we continue to explore the role of curiosity in this chapter, let these historical examples serve as a source of inspiration. Curiosity is not reserved for the great minds of history—it is a trait that resides within all of us, waiting to be awakened and nurtured. By embracing curiosity as the engine of discovery, we embark on a lifelong quest for knowledge that enriches both our understanding of the world and our experience of life itself.

Rekindling Childlike Wonder

Curiosity is one of our most natural traits, evident in the endless questions of a child exploring the world for the first time. Yet, as we grow older, this innate wonder often fades, buried beneath the weight of responsibilities, societal expectations, and the comfort of certainty. Rekindling childlike curiosity is not about regressing to a state of naivety but about rediscovering the joy of asking questions, exploring new ideas, and embracing the unknown. It is an invitation to unlearn rigidity and approach life with a sense of open-mindedness and possibility.

The Beauty of Childlike Curiosity

Children possess a remarkable ability to see the world with fresh eyes. For them, every moment is an opportunity to discover something new, whether it is the way a butterfly moves or the feel of rain on their skin. This unfiltered curiosity is not just endearing—it is foundational to how humans learn and grow.

Consider Albert Einstein's reflection on his own insatiable curiosity: "The important thing is not to stop questioning. Curiosity has its own reason for existing. One cannot help but be in awe when contemplating the mysteries of eternity, of life, of the marvelous structure of reality." Einstein's genius lay not in knowing all the answers but in his willingness to ask questions and challenge assumptions, much like a curious child.

For readers, embracing childlike wonder means granting ourselves permission to marvel at the world again, to let go of the need to have all the answers and instead revel in the joy of seeking them.

Unlearning Rigidity

One of the greatest barriers to curiosity is rigidity—the belief that we already know all we need to know or that there is only one correct way to approach a problem. This mindset often stems from societal conditioning, which prioritizes certainty and expertise over exploration and growth. Over time, this rigidity can stifle creativity and prevent us from seeing new possibilities.

History offers many examples of individuals who overcame rigidity to achieve breakthroughs. One such story is that of Leonardo da Vinci, whose curiosity spanned disciplines from art to anatomy to engineering. Da Vinci's refusal to be confined by conventional wisdom allowed him to see connections others missed, leading to innovations centuries ahead of his time.

To rekindle curiosity, we must first unlearn the habits that limit our thinking. This involves questioning our assumptions, challenging the status quo, and remaining open to perspectives that differ from our own. It is a process of continuous deconstruction and reconstruction, where every question leads to a deeper understanding.

The Power of Open-Mindedness

Open-mindedness is the companion of curiosity, allowing us to entertain new ideas without judgment. It does not require us to agree with every perspective but to consider them with respect and thoughtfulness. Open-mindedness invites us to explore the unfamiliar and embrace uncertainty as a natural part of growth.

The story of Marie Curie exemplifies the power of open-mindedness in action. As a pioneering scientist, Curie faced skepticism and resistance from a field dominated by men. Yet, her willingness to question established norms and pursue unconventional research led to the discovery of radium and polonium, earning her two Nobel

Prizes. Curie's work not only advanced science but also demonstrated the transformative potential of staying open to possibilities others dismissed.

For readers, cultivating open-mindedness involves practicing empathy and curiosity in everyday interactions. By seeking to understand rather than judge, we create space for new ideas and connections to flourish.

The Joy of Exploration

Rekindling childlike wonder also means embracing the joy of exploration—the sense of excitement that comes from venturing into the unknown. This can take many forms, from trying a new hobby to traveling to unfamiliar places to diving into a subject we know little about. The act of exploring not only broadens our horizons but also reawakens our sense of wonder and possibility.

Consider the story of Jacques Cousteau, the legendary oceanographer whose curiosity about the underwater world led to groundbreaking discoveries. Cousteau's explorations were driven not by a desire for fame or fortune but by a deep love for the sea and an insatiable curiosity about its mysteries. His work inspired a generation to care for the oceans, showing how the joy of exploration can lead to profound impact.

For readers, the message is clear: by approaching life as an adventure, we can transform even the mundane into an opportunity for discovery.

Practical Steps to Rekindle Curiosity

Rekindling childlike wonder requires intentional effort. One practical approach is to adopt the mindset of a beginner, even in areas where we have expertise. This involves setting aside preconceived notions and approaching each situation with fresh eyes, as if seeing it for the first time.

Another strategy is to cultivate a habit of asking questions. Children are notorious for their endless "why" questions, a habit that often fades as we grow older. By reintroducing this practice into our lives—asking "Why is this so?" or "What if we tried it differently?"—we reignite our curiosity and uncover new possibilities.

Additionally, surrounding ourselves with curious individuals can be a powerful motivator. The energy and enthusiasm of others can inspire us to explore, question, and learn. Whether through mentorship, collaboration, or simply engaging in meaningful conversations, these connections fuel our own sense of wonder.

The Transformative Impact of Curiosity

Rekindling curiosity is not just about personal fulfillment—it is a transformative force that enriches every aspect of our lives. When we approach the world with curiosity, we become more adaptable, creative, and resilient. We see challenges not as obstacles but as opportunities to learn and grow. We connect more deeply with others, finding common ground in our shared desire to understand and explore.

The poet Rainer Maria Rilke captured this spirit beautifully when he wrote, "Be patient toward all that is unsolved in your heart and try to love the questions themselves." Curiosity invites us to embrace the questions, to live fully in the process of discovery, and to find joy in the journey itself.

A Call to Wonder

As we conclude this section, let us remember that the world is as wondrous as we allow it to be. By unlearning rigidity, embracing open-minded-ness, and nurturing our sense of wonder, we can rekindle the curiosity that drives discovery and enriches our lives. Whether we are exploring the mysteries of the universe or simply marveling at the beauty of a single flower, curiosity connects us to the essence of what it means to be human.

Practical Tools for Lifelong Learning

Curiosity is not a fleeting spark; it is a flame that must be tended and nurtured to burn brightly throughout our lives. While the desire to learn is natural, sustaining it requires intentional effort and practical tools. By incorporating strategies such as reading, asking questions, and explor-ing new hobbies, we can cultivate a mindset of lifelong learning that enriches our understand-ing of the world and empowers us to adapt to its ever-changing landscape.

The Transformative Power of Reading

Few activities feed curiosity as effectively as reading. Books are portals to other worlds, perspectives, and ideas, offering us the chance to explore the depths of human thought and imagination. From philosophy to fiction, science to history, the written word invites us to engage with questions we may never have considered and answers that challenge our assumptions.

Take the example of Theodore Roosevelt, one of America's most intellectually curious presidents. Roosevelt was a voracious reader, devouring books on a wide range of topics, from natural history to military strategy. His curiosity and love of reading informed his policies and personal philosophy, enabling him to lead with both vision and adaptability. For Roosevelt, books were not just a source of knowledge—they were a wellspring of inspiration and growth.

For readers, developing a habit of reading begins with intentionality. Choosing books that pique curiosity and challenge perspectives can spark new ideas and foster a deeper appreciation for the world. Journaling thoughts, questions, and reflections while reading further enhances engagement, transforming a solitary activity into a dynamic dialogue with the text.

The Art of Asking Questions

Curiosity thrives on questions. They are the keys that unlock doors to understanding and the bridges that connect us to new knowledge. From the simple "why" of a child to the probing inquiries of a scientist, questions are the lifeblood of discovery.

One of the greatest proponents of questioning was Socrates, whose method of dialogue relied on asking thought-provoking questions to uncover deeper truths. Socratic questioning encourages critical thinking, self-reflection, and the exploration of assumptions, making it a timeless tool for nurturing curiosity.

In the modern era, innovators like Elon Musk have harnessed the power of questioning to drive breakthroughs. Musk's approach, often referred to as first-principles thinking, involves breaking down complex problems into their fundamental components and asking, "What do we know to be true, and how can we build upon it?" This mindset has propelled advancements in electric vehicles, space exploration, and renewable energy.

For readers, cultivating the art of questioning involves practicing curiosity in everyday interactions. Asking open-ended questions during conversations, seeking to understand rather than to argue, and exploring "what if" scenarios are simple yet powerful ways to keep curiosity alive.

Exploring New Hobbies and Skills

Learning is not confined to books and questions—it also flourishes through hands-on exploration. Engaging in new hobbies and skills invites us to step out of our comfort zones and embrace the joy of experimentation. Whether it's learning a musical instrument, taking up painting, or trying a new sport, hobbies enrich our lives by offering fresh challenges and perspectives.

Consider the story of Julia Child, who discovered her passion for cooking in her late 30s.

What began as a hobby quickly grew into a lifelong pursuit, culminating in her revolutionizing American cuisine with her book *Mastering the Art of French Cooking*. Child's curiosity and willingness to explore a new skill not only transformed her own life but also inspired countless others to embrace the art of cooking.

For readers, exploring new hobbies involves giving oneself permission to be a beginner. It means setting aside the fear of failure and embracing the process of learning for its own sake. The rewards of such exploration are manifold, from enhanced creativity to a greater sense of fulfillment.

Cultivating Curiosity Through Travel and Exploration

Travel is another powerful tool for lifelong learning, offering the chance to encounter new cultures, landscapes, and perspectives. By stepping into unfamiliar environments, we challenge our assumptions and broaden our understanding of the world. Travel does not have to be exotic or expensive to be meaningful—it can be as simple as exploring a nearby town or trying cuisine from a different culture.

The travels of Marco Polo exemplify the transformative power of exploration. His journeys through Asia introduced Europe to new ideas, technologies, and goods, sparking curiosity and innovation across the continent. For readers, adopting a traveler's mindset in daily life—observing the unfamiliar, asking questions, and engaging with new experiences—can cultivate a spirit of curiosity wherever they go.

Leveraging Technology for Lifelong Learning

In today's digital age, technology offers unprecedented opportunities for curiosity and learning. Online courses, virtual museums, podcasts, and discussion forums provide access to knowledge on virtually any topic. Platforms like Khan Academy, Coursera, and TED Talks have democratized education, making it easier than ever to pursue lifelong learning.

However, leveraging technology effectively requires discernment. With the vast amount of information available, it is essential to focus on sources that are credible, engaging, and aligned with personal interests. Setting aside dedicated time for learning and avoiding distractions ensures that technology becomes a tool for growth rather than a source of overwhelm.

The Role of Curiosity in Everyday Life

Lifelong learning is not limited to structured activities—it is a mindset that can be cultivated in daily life. Paying attention to the details of the world around us, engaging in meaningful conversations, and approaching challenges with a sense of curiosity transform the ordinary into the extraordinary.

The naturalist John Muir exemplified this principle. His deep curiosity about nature led him to explore the wilderness with awe and reverence, inspiring the conservation movement and the establishment of national parks. Muir's example reminds us that curiosity need not be grand or complex—it can be as simple as observing the patterns of a leaf or listening to the song of a bird.

For readers, nurturing curiosity in everyday life involves slowing down, noticing the details, and embracing a spirit of wonder. It means asking, "What can I learn from this moment?" and allowing the answer to unfold naturally.

A Journey Without End

Lifelong learning is not a destination—it is a journey, one that unfolds with every question asked, every book read, and every new experience embraced. By incorporating practical tools such as reading, questioning, and exploring, we can keep curiosity alive and thriving. These practices not only deepen our understanding of the world but also enrich our lives with meaning, connection, and growth.

As we continue to explore the role of curiosity in this chapter, let these tools serve as a guide, reminding us that the pursuit of knowledge is a lifelong adventure. In the words of Leonardo da Vinci, "Learning never exhausts the mind." Let us embrace this truth and keep the flame of curiosity burning bright.

Resisting Intellectual Complacency

Curiosity is a dynamic force, constantly propelling us forward. Yet, in a world filled with comfort zones and distractions, the risk of intellectual complacency looms large. Complacency lulls us into a false sense of mastery, convincing us that we know enough or that growth is unnecessary. Resisting this stagnation requires vigilance, adaptability, and a commitment to staying mentally agile in the face of an ever-changing world.

The Dangers of Stagnation

Intellectual complacency often creeps in unnoticed, reinforced by routines and the natural human preference for stability. While routines provide structure, they can also create a mental rut, discouraging exploration and innovation. Over time, this stagnation stifles creativity and leaves individuals ill-equipped to navigate new challenges.

One historical cautionary tale is that of the Ottoman Empire during its decline. Once a center of innovation and learning, the empire became complacent in its power, failing to adapt to advancements in science, technology, and governance emerging in Europe. This resistance to change contributed to its eventual fall, a stark reminder that even the most powerful entities must remain intellectually agile to thrive.

For readers, the lesson is clear: intellectual complacency is not merely a personal issue—it is a universal challenge that affects individuals, organizations, and societies alike. Resisting it begins with an awareness of its subtle but pervasive nature.

Cultivating Mental Agility

Mental agility is the antidote to complacency. It is the ability to adapt to new information, embrace uncertainty, and approach problems with a fresh perspective. Developing this agility requires an intentional effort to challenge assumptions, seek out diverse viewpoints, and remain open to change.

The life of polymath Benjamin Franklin exemplifies mental agility in action. Franklin was not content to excel in a single field; he continually expanded his horizons, delving into science, politics, philosophy, and literature. His curiosity and willingness to reinvent himself allowed him to contribute to the founding of the United

States, the invention of the lightning rod, and countless other achievements.

For readers, Franklin's example underscores the importance of lifelong learning. By diversifying our interests and engaging with new ideas, we not only resist stagnation but also enrich our understanding of the world.

The Role of Discomfort in Growth

Growth rarely occurs in comfort. It is the challenges, uncertainties, and failures that stretch our minds and foster resilience. Embracing discomfort as a natural part of the learning process is essential for staying mentally agile.

Consider the story of Steve Jobs during his time away from Apple. After being ousted from the company he co-founded, Jobs faced a period of uncertainty and reinvention. He went on to create NeXT and acquire Pixar, experiences that ultimately shaped his triumphant return to Apple. Jobs often spoke of the importance of staying hungry and foolish—a mindset that prioritizes growth over comfort and curiosity over complacency.

For readers, the takeaway is that discomfort is not a sign of failure; it is a signal of progress. By leaning into challenges and seeking out experiences that push our boundaries, we cultivate the mental flexibility needed to thrive.

The Impact of Rapid Change

In today's world, the pace of change is accelerating, driven by advancements in technology, shifts in global dynamics, and the proliferation of information. While this rapid change presents opportunities for growth, it also requires constant adaptation. Those who resist change risk falling behind, while those who embrace it position themselves to lead.

One example of successful adaptation is the transformation of Netflix. Originally a DVD rental service, Netflix recognized the shift toward digital streaming and pivoted its business model to become a global leader in entertainment. This willingness to embrace change and innovate exemplifies the agility required to succeed in a rapidly evolving landscape.

For readers, staying mentally agile in the face of change involves cultivating a mindset of curiosity and experimentation. By approaching change with a sense of possibility rather than fear, we can turn challenges into opportunities for growth.

Practical Strategies for Staying Mentally Agile

Resisting intellectual complacency and cultivating mental agility require intentional practices. One effective strategy is to engage in lifelong learning, seeking out new knowledge and skills that challenge and inspire us. This can include taking courses, attending workshops, or exploring unfamiliar subjects through books and discussions.

Another powerful approach is to surround ourselves with diverse perspectives. Engaging with people from different backgrounds, cultures, and disciplines broadens our horizons and exposes us to ideas we might not encounter otherwise. This diversity fosters creativity and helps us navigate complex problems with greater insight.

Finally, embracing a growth mindset is essential. As psychologist Carol Dweck's research demonstrates, individuals who believe in their ability to learn and grow are more likely to persevere through challenges and achieve success. By viewing setbacks as opportunities for growth, we shift our focus from perfection to progress.

A Call to Remain Curious

Intellectual complacency is not a fixed state—it is a choice. By committing to curiosity, adaptability, and lifelong learning, we can resist the pull of stagnation and remain engaged with the world around us. The stories of Franklin, Jobs, and countless others remind us that growth is a journey, not a destination, and that the pursuit of knowledge is one of life's greatest adventures.

As we conclude this chapter, let us reflect on the role of curiosity in shaping our lives and the world. In a rapidly changing world, the ability to stay mentally agile is not just a skill—it is a necessity. Let us embrace the challenge, celebrate the journey, and remain steadfast in our quest for knowledge and growth.

CHAPTER 7: GENIUS AND EMOTIONAL INTELLIGENCE – BALANCING HEART AND MIND

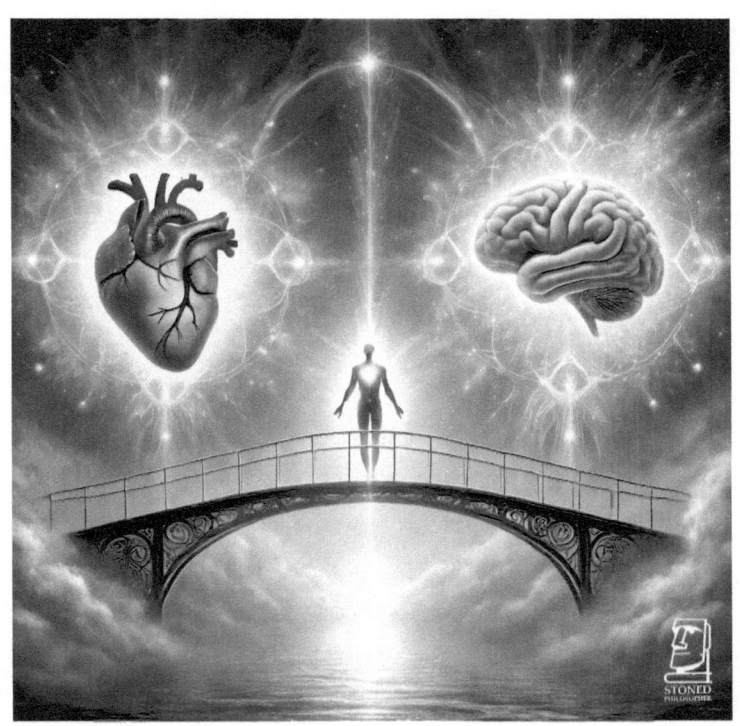

The Interplay Between Emotion and Intellect

The human mind is a marvel of intellectual capacity, capable of unraveling the mysteries of the universe and solving problems of staggering complexity. Yet, intellect alone is not enough to navigate the intricate web of human experience. Emotional intelligence, the ability to understand and manage emotions in ourselves and others, complements intellectual brilliance, creating a balance between heart and mind. This interplay between emotion and intellect is not only the foundation of effective leadership and creativity but also a defining characteristic of true genius.

The Dual Nature of Genius

Genius is often associated with intellectual prowess—a mathematician solving complex equations or an artist revolutionizing their medium. However, history reveals that many of the most impactful figures possessed not just intellectual brilliance but also profound emotional intelligence. They understood that to lead, inspire, and create, one must engage both the mind and the heart.

Mahatma Gandhi, for example, embodied this balance. While his intellect allowed him to craft strategies for India's independence, it was his emotional intelligence that made him a transformative leader. Gandhi's ability to connect with people, empathize with their struggles, and inspire them to embrace nonviolent resistance stemmed from his deep understanding of human emotion. His intellect informed his vision, but his emotional intelligence brought that vision to life, galvanizing a nation and leaving an enduring legacy.

Similarly, Maya Angelou, the celebrated poet and activist, demonstrated the power of emotional intelligence in her work. Her writings, filled with profound insights into the human condition, resonate deeply because they blend intellectual depth with emotional authenticity. Angelou's ability to articulate pain, hope, and resilience in a way that touched millions reflects a genius rooted not only in her mind but also in her heart.

These examples illustrate that emotional intelligence is not a separate or secondary trait—it is an integral part of genius, enhancing and amplifying intellectual abilities.

How Emotion Fuels Intellect

Emotions are often seen as obstacles to rational thought, but they are, in fact, essential to intellectual achievement. Neuroscientist Antonio Damasio's research on decision-making demonstrates that emotions play a critical role in processing information and making choices. Without the guidance of emotions, even the most logical minds struggle to prioritize and act effectively.

The relationship between emotion and intellect is particularly evident in creative endeavors. Artists, writers, and innovators often draw upon their emotional experiences to fuel their work. Vincent van Gogh's masterpieces, for instance, are suffused with the intensity of his emotions, transforming personal struggles into universal expressions of beauty and truth. His intellect guided his technique, but it was his emotional depth that gave his art its power.

For readers, understanding the interplay between emotion and intellect means recognizing that emotions are not a hindrance—they are a source of insight and energy. By embracing and channeling our emotions, we can enhance our intellectual pursuits and connect more deeply with others.

The Synergy of Emotional and Intellectual Intelligence

When emotional and intellectual intelligence work in harmony, they create a synergy that enables individuals to excel in both personal and professional contexts. This synergy is particularly valuable in leadership, where the ability to inspire, motivate, and connect with others is as important as strategic thinking.

Take the example of Jacinda Ardern, the former Prime Minister of New Zealand. Ardern's leadership during crises, such as the Christchurch mosque shootings and the COVID-19 pandemic, demonstrated a rare blend of intellectual acuity and emotional empathy. Her ability to make data-driven decisions while showing genuine compassion for those affected by tragedy earned her widespread admiration and trust.

This synergy also extends to collaboration and teamwork. In the tech industry, Steve Jobs exemplified the fusion of emotion and intellect. While his vision and technical understanding drove Apple's innovation, it was his ability to inspire and challenge his team that brought those ideas to fruition. Jobs's emotional intelligence allowed him to connect with others on a deeper level, fostering creativity and pushing boundaries.

For readers, cultivating this synergy involves developing both intellectual and emotional capacities. It means striving for knowledge while remaining attuned to the emotions that shape our relationships and decisions.

Practical Insights from Emotional Intelligence

To harness the power of emotional intelligence, we must first cultivate self-awareness — the ability to recognize and understand our own emotions. This awareness allows us to manage our emotional responses, preventing them from overwhelming our intellect. Techniques such as mindfulness and reflective journaling can help us tune into our emotions and gain clarity about their impact on our thoughts and actions.

Equally important is the ability to understand and empathize with the emotions of others. Empathy, a cornerstone of emotional intelligence, enables us to build trust, navigate conflicts, and inspire collaboration. By actively listening to others and seeking to understand their perspectives, we strengthen the bonds that make teamwork and leadership effective.

Finally, emotional intelligence requires adaptability—the capacity to respond to changing circumstances with resilience and grace. In a world that is increasingly complex and unpredictable, the ability to navigate uncertainty with both intellect and emotional stability is a hallmark of true genius.

A Call to Balance Heart and Mind

The interplay between emotion and intellect is not a binary choice—it is a dynamic balance that enriches our lives and enhances our impact on the world. By cultivating emotional intelligence alongside intellectual abilities, we unlock the full potential of our genius, enabling us to think critically, connect deeply, and act compassionately.

As we explore the remaining sections of this chapter, let us carry forward the lessons of Gandhi, Angelou, and others who have shown us that true genius lies not in the separation of heart and mind, but in their harmonious integration. In this balance, we find the wisdom to navigate life's complexities and the strength to make a lasting difference.

Understanding and Regulating Emotions

Emotions are an intrinsic part of the human experience, shaping our thoughts, decisions, and actions in profound ways. While they can serve as powerful motivators, unchecked emotions can also lead to impulsive decisions or clouded judgment. Learning to recognize and regulate emotions is essential for unlocking the full potential of our intellectual and creative abilities. By cultivating emotional awareness and control, we gain the clarity and resilience needed to navigate life's complexities with wisdom and grace.

The Importance of Emotional Awareness

Understanding one's emotions begins with awareness—the ability to identify and acknowledge feelings as they arise. This foundational skill allows us to recognize patterns in our emotional responses, uncover their underlying triggers, and assess their impact on our behavior.

Historical figures like Abraham Lincoln exemplify the value of emotional awareness. Known for his steady demeanor and thoughtful decision-making, Lincoln often reflected deeply on his emotions, particularly during moments of great pressure. During the Civil War, his ability to understand and manage his feelings of anger, frustration, and sorrow enabled him to lead the nation with compassion and resolve. Lincoln's emotional self-awareness was not a natural gift but a skill honed through introspection and a commitment to personal growth.

For readers, cultivating emotional awareness requires a willingness to pause and observe our inner state without judgment. Practices such as mindfulness meditation and journaling can help us develop this skill, creating space to reflect on our emotions and their origins.

The Science of Emotional Regulation

Once we become aware of our emotions, the next step is learning to regulate them effectively. Emotional regulation does not mean suppressing or ignoring our feelings—it involves channeling them in ways that serve our goals and values. This process is essential for improving decision-making, enhancing creativity, and maintaining well-being.

Neuroscience offers valuable insights into how we regulate emotions. The prefrontal cortex, responsible for executive functions such as reasoning and planning, plays a crucial role in moderating emotional responses generated by the amygdala, the brain's emotional center. When we encounter a stressful situation, the amygdala may trigger a fight-or-flight response, but the prefrontal cortex helps us assess the situation more rationally and choose an appropriate course of action.

One practical method for regulating emotions is

cognitive reappraisal, a technique that involves reframing our perspective on a situation to reduce its emotional impact. For example, instead of viewing failure as a personal shortcoming, we can reframe it as an opportunity for growth and learning. This shift in perspective not only alleviates negative emotions but also fosters resilience and adaptability.

Emotional Regulation and Creativity

Emotional regulation is particularly important in creative pursuits, where the ability to balance intense emotions with focused effort can lead to breakthroughs. Many of history's greatest creators and innovators have demonstrated this balance, channeling their emotional energy into their work while maintaining clarity of thought.

Frida Kahlo, the renowned Mexican artist, transformed her physical and emotional pain into powerful works of art that continue to resonate with audiences worldwide. Her ability to confront and express her emotions through her paintings allowed her to create pieces that were both deeply personal and universally relatable. Kahlo's story illustrates that regulating emotions does not mean avoiding them—it means finding constructive ways to process and express them.

For readers, emotional regulation in creativity involves embracing emotions as a source of inspiration while setting boundaries to prevent them from overwhelming the creative process. Techniques such as setting aside dedicated time for reflection or engaging in mindfulness practices can help maintain this balance.

Tools for Emotional Regulation

Developing emotional regulation is a lifelong practice that requires consistent effort and self-compassion. One effective tool is deep breathing, a simple yet powerful technique for calming the nervous system during moments of stress. By focusing on slow, intentional breaths, we activate the parasympathetic nervous system, which helps reduce the intensity of emotional responses.

Another valuable approach is practicing gratitude. By intentionally focusing on the positive aspects of our lives, we can shift our emotional state and cultivate a sense of contentment and perspective. Research has shown that gratitude practices, such as keeping a gratitude journal, can enhance emotional well-being and resilience.

Additionally, seeking support from trusted individuals can be instrumental in regulating emotions. Sharing our feelings with friends, family, or mentors not only provides relief but also offers new perspectives that can help us navigate challenges more effectively.

The Interplay of Emotion and Decision-Making

Emotional regulation plays a crucial role in decision-making, where unchecked emotions can lead to impulsive or irrational choices. By managing our emotions, we create the mental clarity needed to weigh options, consider consequences, and make decisions aligned with our long-term goals.

Warren Buffett, one of the most successful investors of all time, is a master of emotional regulation in decision-making. Buffett's ability to

remain calm and rational during market fluctu-
ations has been a key factor in his success. He
often emphasizes the importance of emotional
discipline, reminding others that "emotions are
the enemy of good decisions."

For readers, adopting a deliberate and reflective
approach to decision-making can help minimize the influence of fleeting emotions. Taking
a moment to step back, assess the situation, and
consult trusted advisors can lead to wiser and
more thoughtful choices.

A Path to Empowerment

Understanding and regulating emotions is not
about suppressing what makes us human—it
is about harnessing our emotional energy in
ways that empower us to thrive. By cultivating emotional awareness, practicing regulation
techniques, and embracing the interplay of
emotion and intellect, we unlock the potential
to navigate life's challenges with wisdom and
creativity.

As we move forward in this chapter, let us carry
with us the knowledge that emotional intel-

ligence is not a fixed trait but a skill that can be developed and refined. By committing to this practice, we not only enhance our personal growth but also create a foundation for deeper connections, greater resilience, and lasting fulfillment.

Building Empathy and Social Awareness

Empathy, often described as the ability to understand and share the feelings of others, is a cornerstone of emotional intelligence. It bridges the gap between individuals, fostering connection and understanding in a way that transcends intellectual reasoning alone. Combined with social awareness—the capacity to navigate social dynamics with insight and sensitivity—empathy enhances collaboration, strengthens leadership, and inspires action. Together, these qualities form a powerful foundation for achieving both personal and collective goals.

The Transformative Power of Empathy

Empathy is not merely a soft skill; it is a transformative force that drives meaningful human connection and effective problem-solving. Throughout history, empathetic leaders and thinkers have demonstrated the profound impact of understanding others' experiences and perspectives.

Consider Eleanor Roosevelt, one of the most empathetic figures in modern history. As First Lady of the United States during the Great Depression and World War II, Roosevelt devoted herself to understanding the struggles of ordinary citizens. She visited factories, spoke with workers, and listened to their concerns firsthand, often challenging her own preconceived notions. Her deep empathy informed her advocacy for human rights and social justice, earning her the title "First Lady of the World." Roosevelt's story illustrates how empathy can inspire leadership that is both compassionate and impactful.

For readers, empathy begins with the simple act of listening—not just hearing words, but truly seeking to understand the emotions and motivations behind them. By practicing active listening, we open ourselves to new perspectives and build the trust necessary for meaningful collaboration.

Empathy as the Key to Collaboration

In the context of collaboration, empathy enables individuals to work together harmoniously, even in the face of differing opinions and approaches. It fosters an environment where all voices are heard and valued, creating the psychological safety necessary for innovation and problem-solving.

The success of the Apollo 11 moon landing provides a striking example of empathy-driven collaboration. Engineers, scientists, and astronauts from diverse backgrounds worked together toward a common goal, often navigating intense challenges and high-stakes decisions. Empathy allowed these teams to communicate effectively, resolve conflicts, and maintain focus on their shared mission. This achievement underscores the importance of understanding and valuing others' contributions in a collaborative setting.

For readers, empathy in teamwork involves recognizing the unique strengths and perspectives each individual brings to the table. By approaching interactions with curiosity and respect, we create a culture of inclusivity and cooperation that maximizes collective potential.

The Role of Empathy in Leadership

Empathy is particularly critical in leadership, where the ability to inspire and guide others depends on understanding their needs, aspirations, and challenges. Empathetic leaders do not merely command; they connect, creating a sense of shared purpose and motivation.

Martin Luther King Jr. exemplified empathetic leadership in his fight for civil rights. King's speeches and actions were deeply rooted in his understanding of the injustices faced by marginalized communities. His empathy allowed him to articulate their struggles with authenticity and passion, inspiring millions to join the movement for equality and justice. King's ability to connect with others on an emotional level made him not only a powerful orator but also a unifying force for change.

For readers aspiring to lead, empathy involves more than acknowledging others' emotions— it requires action. By demonstrating genuine care and taking steps to address the concerns of those we lead, we cultivate loyalty, trust, and a shared commitment to achieving goals.

Developing Social Awareness

While empathy focuses on individual connections, social awareness expands this understanding to broader dynamics, including cultural norms, group interactions, and organizational structures. Socially aware individuals possess a keen sense of how their actions and words influence others, allowing them to navigate complex social environments with grace and effectiveness.

Malala Yousafzai, the Nobel Prize-winning activist for girls' education, exemplifies social awareness in action. Yousafzai's advocacy is rooted in her deep understanding of the cultural and societal barriers faced by girls in her native Pakistan and around the world. Her ability to communicate these challenges to a global audience has mobilized support and inspired change, demonstrating the power of social awareness to bridge divides and foster collective action.

For readers, cultivating social awareness involves paying attention to the unspoken dynamics of interactions. Observing body language, tone of voice, and group behavior provides valuable insights into how others perceive and respond to situations. This awareness enhances our ability to adapt our communication and actions to align with the needs of those around us.

Practical Strategies for Building Empathy and Social Awareness

Developing empathy and social awareness is a continuous process that requires intention and practice. One effective approach is to engage in perspective-taking—imagining oneself in another person's situation to better understand their feelings and motivations. This practice not only enhances empathy but also reduces biases and fosters greater compassion.

Another powerful tool is storytelling. Sharing and listening to personal stories deepens our emotional connection with others, creating a sense of shared humanity. Stories have the unique ability to transcend barriers and evoke empathy, making them an invaluable resource for building social awareness.

Finally, seeking diverse experiences and interactions broadens our understanding of the world and the people in it. Traveling, volunteering, and participating in multicultural events expose us to different perspectives, enriching our capacity for empathy and social awareness.

Empathy and Inspiration

Empathy not only enhances collaboration and leadership but also inspires others to act with purpose and compassion. When we understand and connect with others on a deep level, we create a ripple effect of kindness and understanding that extends far beyond our immediate interactions.

The legacy of figures like Eleanor Roosevelt, Martin Luther King Jr., and Malala Yousafzai reminds us that empathy is not a passive quality—it is a force for change. By cultivating empathy and social awareness in our own lives, we become agents of positive transformation, inspiring others to join us in building a more compassionate and connected world.

A Call to Empathy

As we conclude this section, let us reflect on the power of empathy and social awareness to shape our relationships, communities, and society at large. By striving to understand and uplift those around us, we not only enhance our own emotional intelligence but also contribute to a world where collaboration and connection thrive.

In the words of Maya Angelou, "People will forget what you said, people will forget what you did, but people will never forget how you made them feel." Let this truth guide us as we seek to balance heart and mind in our journey toward genius.

Emotional Resilience and Genius

Emotional resilience is the quiet strength that allows individuals to weather life's storms and emerge not only intact but often stronger. It is a hallmark of genius, underpinning the ability to navigate challenges, adapt to change, and sustain focus on long-term goals. While intellect and creativity fuel achievement, it is emotional resilience that provides the endurance and stability necessary to see ambitions through to fruition.

The Essence of Emotional Resilience

At its core, emotional resilience is the capacity to recover from setbacks and maintain a sense of purpose and equilibrium. It is not the absence of adversity but the ability to face adversity with courage and determination. This quality is particularly crucial for those who aspire to greatness, as the pursuit of ambitious goals inevitably involves obstacles, failures, and moments of doubt.

History offers countless examples of individuals whose emotional resilience was instrumental in their success. One such figure is Thomas Edison, whose path to inventing the electric lightbulb was marked by repeated failures. Edison famously remarked, "I have not failed. I've just found 10,000 ways that won't work." His ability to reframe setbacks as opportunities for learning exemplifies the resilience that underpinned his genius. For Edison, failure was not a destination but a stepping stone toward innovation.

Resilience in the Face of Criticism

Emotional resilience also enables individuals to endure criticism and rejection, which are often inevitable companions to originality and ambition. Visionaries and innovators frequently encounter skepticism, resistance, and ridicule, yet their resilience allows them to remain steadfast in their convictions.

The life of J.K. Rowling illustrates this principle. Before achieving global success with the *Harry Potter* series, Rowling faced a series of personal and professional setbacks, including multiple rejections from publishers. Her ability to persevere despite these challenges and maintain her belief in her story was a testament to her emotional resilience. Today, her work stands as a cultural phenomenon, inspiring millions around the world.

For readers, resilience in the face of criticism requires a mindset that values progress over perfection. By viewing criticism as an opportunity for growth and focusing on the larger vision, we can navigate challenges with greater confidence and clarity.

The Link Between Resilience and Long-Term Focus

Genius often requires sustained effort over extended periods, a feat that demands not only intellectual stamina but also emotional resilience. Long-term focus is particularly challenging in an era of constant distractions and instant gratification, yet it remains a critical component of meaningful achievement.

Consider the story of Marie Curie, who spent years conducting painstaking research that ultimately led to the discovery of radium and polonium. Her resilience in the face of scientific uncertainty, financial difficulties, and personal tragedy allowed her to maintain focus on her goals. Curie's unwavering dedication to her work exemplifies the interplay between resilience and sustained focus, a combination that defines true genius.

For readers, cultivating long-term focus involves setting clear goals, maintaining perspective, and building habits that support resilience. Practices such as mindfulness, reflection, and regular self-care can provide the emotional foundation needed to persevere through challenges.

The Role of Adaptability in Resilience

Emotional resilience is not static; it is a dynamic quality that evolves in response to changing circumstances. Adaptability—the ability to adjust to new challenges and opportunities—is a key component of resilience, allowing individuals to thrive in the face of uncertainty.

Nelson Mandela's life offers a profound example of adaptability and resilience. During his 27 years of imprisonment, Mandela endured immense hardship, yet he emerged with a vision for reconciliation and unity that transformed South Africa. His ability to adapt to his circumstances and channel his experiences into a greater purpose exemplifies the resilience that characterizes extraordinary leadership.

For readers, developing adaptability involves cultivating a growth mindset and remaining open to change. By viewing challenges as opportunities for growth and embracing the un-known, we can build the flexibility and strength needed to navigate life's twists and turns.

Practical Strategies for Building Resilience

Emotional resilience is not an innate trait but a skill that can be developed and strengthened over time. One effective strategy is to reframe challenges as opportunities for growth. This shift in perspective not only reduces the emotional burden of setbacks but also fosters a pro-active approach to problem-solving.

Another powerful tool is cultivating a strong support network. Resilient individuals often draw strength from their relationships, seeking encouragement, advice, and perspective from trusted friends, family, and mentors. Building and maintaining these connections provides a vital foundation for navigating adversity.

Additionally, prioritizing self-care is essential for resilience. Physical and emotional well-be-ing are deeply interconnected, and practices such as exercise, healthy eating, and adequate rest contribute to greater emotional stability and strength.

A Legacy of Resilience

Emotional resilience is not only a personal virtue but also a legacy that inspires others. Figures like Edison, Rowling, Curie, and Mandela remind us that resilience is the bridge between ambition and achievement, enabling individuals to overcome obstacles and realize their potential. Their stories challenge us to cultivate resilience in our own lives, turning setbacks into stepping stones and challenges into opportunities.

A Call to Resilience

As we conclude this section, let us reflect on the role of emotional resilience in achieving greatness. Genius is not merely a matter of intellect or talent—it is the ability to persevere, adapt, and maintain focus in the face of adversity. By cultivating resilience, we unlock the strength to pursue our dreams with courage and determination, leaving a legacy that inspires others to do the same.

In the words of Maya Angelou, "I can be

changed by what happens to me, but I refuse to be reduced by it." Let this truth guide us as we strive to balance heart and mind, embracing the challenges that shape our journey toward genius.

CHAPTER 8: UNLOCKING YOUR GENIUS – A BLUEPRINT FOR GREATNESS

Synthesizing the Lessons

Genius, as explored throughout this book, is not an unattainable gift bestowed upon a select few but a dynamic quality that emerges from the interplay of curiosity, focus, emotional intelligence, collaboration, and resilience. It is a journey shaped by the deliberate cultivation of habits, mindsets, and principles that align our inner potential with the challenges and opportunities of the world around us. As we approach the culmination of this exploration, it is time to synthesize these themes, weaving them into a cohesive blueprint for unlocking genius in everyday life.

The Nature of Genius as Integration

At its core, genius is the ability to harmonize diverse elements of the self—intellect, emotion, imagination, and perseverance—into a force that drives creativity and achievement. History's greatest minds, from Leonardo da Vinci to Maya Angelou, exemplify this integration. They combined intellectual rigor with emotional depth, curiosity with resilience, and vision with practical execution, creating a symphony of traits that allowed them to transcend conventional limits.

Leonardo da Vinci, for instance, epitomized the integration of curiosity and focus. His insatiable desire to understand the natural world led him to explore anatomy, physics, and art, while his disciplined focus enabled him to create masterpieces such as *The Last Supper* and *Vitruvian Man*. For readers, Leonardo's life underscores the importance of synthesizing these traits to pursue greatness in any domain.

The Role of Curiosity in Igniting Genius

Curiosity serves as the spark that ignites the journey toward genius. It fuels our desire to explore, question, and learn, breaking down the barriers of complacency and opening the door to discovery. From Galileo's quest to understand the cosmos to Richard Feynman's playful exploration of the quantum world, curiosity has driven humanity's greatest achievements.

Yet curiosity alone is not enough—it must be paired with focus and discipline to transform raw interest into meaningful outcomes. As we reflect on the lessons of this book, it becomes clear that curiosity provides the energy, but focus channels that energy into purposeful action.

Focus as the Driver of Mastery

While curiosity invites us to explore the breadth of knowledge, focus allows us to delve deeply, mastering the skills and concepts necessary for transformative impact. Michelangelo's unwavering dedication to the Sistine Chapel and Marie Curie's tireless pursuit of scientific discovery exemplify the power of sustained focus in achieving greatness.

Focus is not merely about concentration; it is about aligning our efforts with our highest priorities and resisting the distractions that dilute our potential. As modern readers, we are challenged to cultivate deep work habits, creating the space and structure needed to immerse ourselves fully in our pursuits.

Emotional Intelligence: Balancing Heart and Mind

Genius is not an isolated intellectual endeavor—it is deeply connected to our emotions and relationships. Emotional intelligence, which encompasses self-awareness, empathy, and resilience, enhances our ability to collaborate, lead, and inspire.

Figures like Gandhi and Eleanor Roosevelt demonstrate how emotional intelligence amplifies genius. Gandhi's ability to connect with the struggles of millions and channel their collective aspirations into a movement for independence exemplifies the transformative power of empathy and social awareness. For readers, developing emotional intelligence involves not only understanding our own emotions but also building bridges of connection and trust with others.

The Collaborative Nature of Genius

Genius often flourishes in the context of collaboration, where the diverse perspectives and talents of individuals come together to achieve shared goals. The success of the Manhattan Project, the Apollo 11 moon landing, and even The Beatles' musical legacy illustrates how collective effort amplifies individual genius.

Collaboration is not about diminishing our individuality but about leveraging our unique strengths within a larger framework of teamwork. By cultivating trust, communication, and mutual respect, we create environments where genius can thrive—both our own and that of those around us.

Resilience: The Foundation of Endurance

Every journey toward genius encounters obstacles, failures, and moments of doubt. Resilience, the ability to adapt and persevere, provides the foundation for enduring these challenges and continuing forward.

Thomas Edison's countless experiments before perfecting the lightbulb and J.K. Rowling's rejections before publishing *Harry Potter* illustrate the critical role of resilience in achieving greatness. For readers, resilience is not just about enduring hardship—it is about reframing setbacks as opportunities for growth and maintaining a long-term perspective.

The Interconnected Path to Genius

As we synthesize these themes, a clear pattern emerges: genius is not a linear trait but a multidimensional process. It is the integration of curiosity, focus, emotional intelligence, collaboration, and resilience that creates a holistic path to greatness. Each of these elements supports and reinforces the others, forming a dynamic system that adapts to the challenges and opportunities of life.

For example, curiosity sparks the desire to explore new ideas, while focus channels that exploration into mastery. Emotional intelligence enhances our ability to collaborate and build relationships, which in turn fosters resilience by providing support and perspective. This interconnected framework offers readers a practical blueprint for cultivating genius in their own lives.

Applying the Lessons

Synthesizing these lessons is only the first step; the true power of this knowledge lies in its application. Each reader's journey toward genius will be unique, shaped by their goals, passions, and circumstances. By embracing the principles outlined in this book and tailoring them to their individual needs, readers can create a personalized path to greatness.

As we transition to the next sections of this chapter, we will explore practical strategies for applying these lessons, cultivating a growth-oriented lifestyle, and answering the call to greatness. For now, let us reflect on the profound truth that genius is not a destination but a journey—one that is open to all who are willing to embark on it.

Developing a Personalized Framework

Every journey toward genius is as unique as the individual embarking on it. The principles outlined in this book—curiosity, focus, emotional intelligence, collaboration, and resilience—offer a universal foundation, but their application must be tailored to the aspirations, strengths, and circumstances of each reader. Creating a personalized framework is not about rigidly adhering to a prescribed formula; it is about crafting a dynamic and adaptable plan that evolves with your growth and goals.

The Starting Point: Self-Awareness

Developing a personalized framework begins with self-awareness. This foundational step requires an honest evaluation of your passions, values, strengths, and areas for improvement. Self-awareness is not a destination but a continuous process of reflection and discovery, allowing you to align your actions with your authentic self.

Socrates, the ancient Greek philosopher, famously declared, "Know thyself." For him, self-awareness was the cornerstone of wisdom and personal growth. Today, this principle remains just as relevant. By understanding your motivations and tendencies, you can identify the elements of genius that resonate most strongly with your aspirations.

For readers, practical self-awareness exercises include journaling, seeking feedback from trusted mentors or peers, and engaging in mindfulness practices. These activities provide valuable insights into your inner landscape, forming the foundation for your personalized framework.

Clarifying Your Vision

Once you have a clearer understanding of yourself, the next step is to define your vision. This vision serves as a guiding star, inspiring and directing your efforts. It should be both ambitious and grounded in reality—a balance that allows you to dream big while taking actionable steps toward your goals.

Consider the story of Oprah Winfrey, whose vision of empowering others shaped her career and legacy. Despite facing significant challenges in her early life, Winfrey's clarity of purpose allowed her to harness her strengths and navigate obstacles with determination. Her vision became the driving force behind her success, demonstrating the transformative power of aligning one's efforts with a meaningful purpose.

For readers, clarifying your vision involves asking questions such as: What impact do I want to make? What inspires me to take action? How do I define success? These reflections help you craft a vision that is uniquely yours, setting the stage for meaningful growth.

Building Your Framework

With self-awareness and a clear vision in place, the next step is to construct your framework. This involves translating the principles of genius into actionable strategies and practices that fit your lifestyle and goals.

1. Curiosity as the Foundation

Begin by fostering a mindset of curiosity. Identify areas of interest and commit to exploring them with an open mind. Whether through reading, attending workshops, or engaging in discussions, curiosity fuels the learning and experimentation that drive progress.

2. Focus as the Driver

Create habits and routines that support deep work and sustained focus. This might involve setting aside dedicated time for creative pursuits, minimizing distractions, and prioritizing tasks that align with your vision. Remember that focus is not just about intensity; it is about consistency and persistence.

3. Emotional Intelligence as the Bridge

Incorporate practices that enhance self-aware-ness, empathy, and emotional regulation. These skills not only improve your interactions with others but also strengthen your ability to navi-gate challenges and maintain balance.

4. Collaboration as the Amplifier

Seek opportunities to collaborate with others who share your values and goals. Whether through partnerships, mentorships, or team-work, collaboration allows you to leverage col-lective strengths and achieve outcomes greater than the sum of their parts.

5. Resilience as the Foundation of Growth

Cultivate resilience by reframing setbacks as opportunities for learning. Develop strategies for managing stress and adversity, such as prac-ticing mindfulness, building a support network, and maintaining a growth mindset.

Adapting Your Framework Over Time

A personalized framework is not static—it evolves as you gain new insights and encounter changing circumstances. Periodic reflection and assessment are essential for ensuring that your plan remains aligned with your vision and goals.

Steve Jobs's career provides a compelling example of adaptability. After being ousted from Apple, he used the experience to reinvent himself, founding NeXT and acquiring Pixar. When he returned to Apple years later, his vision had matured, and he was able to lead the company to unprecedented success. Jobs's ability to adapt his framework in response to life's twists and turns highlights the importance of flexibility in pursuing greatness.

For readers, regular check-ins with your framework can help you stay on track and make adjustments as needed. Ask yourself: Are my strategies still effective? Have my goals or priorities shifted? What new opportunities or challenges have emerged? This process of reflection ensures that your framework remains a living, breathing tool for growth.

Balancing Ambition and Well-Being

As you implement your framework, it is crucial to balance ambition with well-being. The pursuit of genius should not come at the expense of your physical, emotional, or mental health. Instead, it should enhance your overall quality of life, fostering a sense of purpose and fulfillment.

The life of Viktor Frankl, a Holocaust survivor and author of *Man's Search for Meaning*, offers profound insights into this balance. Frankl's philosophy centered on finding meaning in even the most challenging circumstances, emphasizing that purpose and well-being are deeply interconnected. For readers, this means prioritizing self-care and maintaining perspective as you work toward your goals.

A Blueprint for Greatness

Your personalized framework is not just a plan— it is a blueprint for greatness, a dynamic map that guides you toward realizing your potential.

By integrating the principles of curiosity, focus, emotional intelligence, collaboration, and resilience, you create a path that is uniquely yours, grounded in authenticity and purpose.

As we continue to explore the final sections of this chapter, let us remember that the journey toward genius is not about perfection—it is about progress. With a personalized framework in hand, you are equipped to navigate life's challenges, embrace its opportunities, and unlock the full spectrum of your potential.

Cultivating a Growth-Oriented Lifestyle

The path to unlocking genius is not a single leap but a continuous journey, sustained by the deliberate cultivation of habits, mindset shifts, and purposeful goal-setting. A growth-oriented lifestyle is not merely about achieving milestones; it is about embracing the process of becoming—a daily commitment to learning, evolving, and expanding the boundaries of your potential. By creating an environment and mindset conducive to growth, we transform ambition into sustainable progress.

The Power of Daily Habits

Habits form the backbone of a growth-oriented lifestyle. These small, consistent actions compound over time, shaping who we are and what we achieve. Greatness is not born in moments of inspiration but in the quiet discipline of daily effort.

Consider the life of Benjamin Franklin, one of history's most celebrated polymaths. Franklin famously developed a personal framework of virtues and daily practices designed to foster growth and self-improvement. Each day, he reflected on his actions, assessed his adherence to these principles, and adjusted his approach as needed. This methodical commitment to growth allowed him to excel in diverse fields, from science to politics to literature.

For readers, adopting growth-oriented habits involves starting small and focusing on consistency. Whether it is setting aside time for deep work, journaling reflections, or practicing mindfulness, the key is to create routines that align with your vision and values.

Mindset Shifts: Embracing Growth

A growth-oriented lifestyle begins with the mind. Shifting from a fixed mindset to a growth mindset—a concept popularized by psychologist Carol Dweck—is essential for unlocking potential. A fixed mindset views abilities as static, while a growth mindset embraces the belief that talents and intelligence can be developed through effort and learning.

The life of Helen Keller exemplifies the transformative power of a growth mindset. Despite the challenges of being blind and deaf from a young age, Keller pursued education with unwavering determination, guided by her teacher Anne Sullivan. Keller's resilience and commitment to growth enabled her to become an author, activist, and global symbol of human potential.

For readers, cultivating a growth mindset involves reframing challenges as opportunities, valuing effort over immediate success, and embracing feedback as a tool for improvement. This mental shift not only enhances personal growth but also fosters resilience and adaptability in the face of adversity.

The Role of Goal-Setting in Sustaining Growth

Goal-setting provides direction and purpose, transforming abstract aspirations into actionable steps. Effective goals are both ambitious and attainable, striking a balance that motivates progress without leading to burnout. They serve as markers of growth, reminding us of our purpose and measuring our progress along the way.

John F. Kennedy's challenge to land a man on the moon within a decade illustrates the power of goal-setting. The ambitious vision united scientists, engineers, and policymakers in pursuit of a common purpose, ultimately leading to one of humanity's most remarkable achievements. For readers, setting clear, meaningful goals creates a sense of focus and determination that propels growth.

A practical approach to goal-setting involves breaking larger ambitions into smaller, actionable steps. This method, often referred to as "chunking," allows us to tackle challenges incrementally, maintaining momentum and motivation. Regularly reviewing and adjusting goals ensures they remain aligned with our evolving vision.

Creating a Growth-Oriented Environment

A growth-oriented lifestyle extends beyond individual habits and mindset—it also involves shaping our environment to support progress. Surrounding ourselves with inspiring people, resources, and spaces fosters an atmosphere of curiosity and innovation.

The salons of the Enlightenment era offer a historical example of this principle. These gatherings of intellectuals, writers, and thinkers created an environment where ideas flourished and collaborations thrived. Figures like Voltaire, Rousseau, and Mary Wollstonecraft benefited from the stimulating exchanges that took place in these settings.

For readers, cultivating a growth-oriented environment might involve joining communities of like-minded individuals, curating a library of inspiring books, or creating a workspace that encourages focus and creativity. These intentional choices reinforce the habits and mindset that drive growth.

The Balance Between Ambition and Rest

Sustaining personal growth requires balance. While ambition and effort are vital, they must be tempered with periods of rest and renewal. Growth is not a sprint; it is a marathon, and pacing oneself is essential for long-term success.

The Japanese concept of *kaizen*, or continuous improvement, embodies this balance. Rooted in the philosophy of making small, consistent improvements, *kaizen* emphasizes progress without overwhelming effort. It reminds us that growth is a process of steady evolution, not relentless striving.

For readers, incorporating rest into a growth-oriented lifestyle involves prioritizing self-care, recognizing the value of downtime, and celebrating incremental progress. These practices ensure that growth remains sustainable and fulfilling.

A Lifelong Commitment to Growth

A growth-oriented lifestyle is not a phase or a project—it is a lifelong commitment to becoming the best version of yourself. It requires patience, persistence, and a willingness to embrace the unknown. Yet, the rewards of this journey are profound: a deeper sense of purpose, a greater capacity for creativity and resilience, and the fulfillment of realizing your potential.

The story of lifelong learner Leonardo da Vinci reminds us that growth has no endpoint. Even in his final days, Leonardo continued to ask questions, explore new ideas, and challenge his own understanding of the world. His insatiable curiosity and dedication to improvement serve as a timeless inspiration for anyone committed to growth.

For readers, the journey toward genius is not about achieving perfection—it is about embracing progress. By cultivating daily habits, adopting a growth mindset, setting meaningful goals, and creating a supportive environment, we lay the foundation for a life of continual evolution.

The Call to Greatness

Every person carries within them a spark of genius—a unique potential waiting to be realized. Yet, the journey toward greatness is not a passive one. It requires courage, intention, and action. As we conclude this exploration of genius, let us issue a call to greatness: a challenge to rise beyond self-imposed limitations, embrace the principles of genius, and take bold steps toward unlocking the extraordinary potential within.

The Courage to Begin

Greatness begins with a single step: the decision to try. It is easy to be paralyzed by fear or doubt, to convince ourselves that we are not ready or worthy. But history reminds us that genius often arises not from perfection but from persistence.

Consider the story of Vincent van Gogh. In his lifetime, he sold only a single painting, enduring poverty and criticism that might have crushed a less resilient spirit. Yet van Gogh continued to paint, driven by an unrelenting desire to express his vision. Today, his works are celebrated as masterpieces, a testament to the enduring impact of courage and dedication.

For readers, the courage to begin is the first step in answering the call to greatness. It is the willingness to take imperfect action, to stumble and rise again, to embrace the process of growth with open arms.

Claiming Responsibility for Your Potential

Unlocking your genius is not a task for others—it is a responsibility that rests with you alone. While external factors and circumstances shape our lives, the ultimate power to transform lies within us. This truth is both liberating and daunting, for it challenges us to take ownership of our journey.

Oprah Winfrey's life exemplifies the power of taking responsibility for one's potential. Born into poverty and facing immense adversity, Winfrey could have accepted her circumstances as insurmountable. Instead, she chose to harness her inner strength, building a career that has inspired millions. Her success is not just a story of talent but of accountability—a reminder that greatness is a choice we make every day.

For readers, claiming responsibility means rejecting excuses and embracing agency. It is the recognition that while we cannot control every aspect of life, we can choose how we respond and what we create.

The Role of Bold Action

Genius is not a static quality; it is revealed through action. The principles outlined in this book—curiosity, focus, emotional intelligence, collaboration, and resilience—are not abstract concepts but practical tools that come to life through use. To unlock your genius, you must act boldly, taking steps that align with your vision and values.

The story of Harriet Tubman illustrates the transformative power of bold action. Born into slavery, Tubman escaped to freedom but did not stop there. She returned to the South repeatedly, risking her life to lead others to freedom through the Underground Railroad. Tubman's courage and unwavering commitment to her mission embody the essence of greatness: the willingness to take action in pursuit of a higher purpose.

For readers, bold action might mean pursuing a long-held dream, advocating for change, or simply stepping out of their comfort zone. It is not the magnitude of the action that matters but the intention and courage behind it.

Inspiring Others Through Your Journey

Genius is not a solitary pursuit—it is a force that inspires and uplifts those around us. When we answer the call to greatness, we create a ripple effect, encouraging others to do the same. Our actions, however small, have the power to ignite change and foster a culture of growth and possibility.

Rosa Parks's quiet defiance on a Montgomery bus in 1955 serves as a poignant example of how individual courage can inspire collective action. By refusing to give up her seat, Parks sparked a movement that changed the course of history. Her story reminds us that greatness is not measured by fame or fortune but by the impact we have on others.

For readers, the call to greatness is not just a

personal journey—it is an invitation to lead by example. By living authentically and pursuing their potential, they inspire others to do the same, creating a legacy of courage and growth.

A Vision of What is Possible

Greatness is not reserved for the extraordinary; it is available to all who are willing to reach for it. The principles of genius outlined in this book are not constraints but invitations—a blueprint for realizing the unique potential within each of us.

Imagine a world where more individuals embrace their genius, contributing their creativity, compassion, and resilience to the collective good. Such a world is not a distant dream but a possibility that begins with each of us. By answering the call to greatness, we not only transform our own lives but also contribute to a better future for all.

A Final Charge

As we close this chapter, let us return to the words of Maya Angelou: "You may not control all the events that happen to you, but you can decide not to be reduced by them." Genius is not about avoiding challenges but about rising to meet them, using every experience as an opportunity to grow and create.

To the reader: You hold within you the spark of genius. You have the tools, the principles, and the potential to create a life of purpose and impact. The path will not always be easy, but it will always be worth it. Take the first step, and then the next. Trust in your ability to learn, adapt, and thrive.

The world needs your brilliance, your vision, and your courage. The call to greatness has been issued. Will you answer it?

CONCLUSION: A JOURNEY TOWARD GENIUS

The journey of genius is, above all, a journey of becoming. It is a process of embracing the fullness of our potential and using it to create something meaningful, both for ourselves and the world around us. This book has explored the many dimensions of genius—curiosity, focus, emotional intelligence, collaboration, resilience, and vision—not as isolated traits but as inter-connected principles that form a cohesive path toward greatness.

As we close this exploration, let us take a moment to reflect on the lessons shared and how they intertwine to illuminate a singular truth: genius is not a gift reserved for the select few but a quality that resides within each of us, waiting to be awakened. It is the spark of creativity, the courage to persevere, and the commitment to grow that ultimately define who we are and what we leave behind.

The Power of Choice

One of the most empowering realizations we can take from this journey is that genius is a choice. It is the decision to be curious in the face of uncertainty, to focus amid distractions, and to remain resilient in the wake of setbacks. It is the choice to connect deeply with others, to act boldly in pursuit of our vision, and to never stop growing.

This understanding shifts the narrative from one of passivity to one of empowerment. We are not bound by the circumstances of our birth, the opinions of others, or the challenges we face. Instead, we hold the power to shape our lives, step by step, through the principles of genius.

Consider the lives of the great thinkers, creators, and leaders who have inspired these pages. Their stories remind us that genius is not a static trait but a dynamic process of becoming. From the perseverance of Thomas Edison to the empathy of Eleanor Roosevelt, the curiosity of Leonardo da Vinci to the resilience of Nelson Mandela, we see that genius is not a singular quality but a mosaic of choices, actions, and values.

The Principles of Genius in Everyday Life

As we move forward, the challenge is not simply to admire these principles but to live them. Each chapter of this book has offered insights and tools to help you unlock your potential, but their true power lies in their application. Let us revisit these principles briefly to see how they can shape the rhythm of our daily lives:

- **Curiosity:** Let it guide you to explore new ideas, ask questions, and seek understanding in even the most mundane moments. Embrace the wonder of the world and let it inspire you to grow.

- **Focus:** Create space for deep work and sustained effort. Eliminate distractions, prioritize your goals, and commit to the work that matters most to you.

- **Emotional Intelligence:** Cultivate self-awareness, empathy, and resilience. Build meaningful connections with others and navigate challenges with grace and adaptability.

- **Collaboration:** Seek out partnerships and communities that amplify your strengths and broaden your perspective. Recognize the power of collective effort to achieve extraordinary results.

- **Resilience:** Reframe setbacks as opportunities for growth. Develop the strength to persevere through adversity and the flexibility to adapt to change.

- **Vision:** Align your actions with your values and purpose. Let your vision serve as a guiding star, inspiring bold action and sustained effort.

Together, these principles create a holistic framework for living with intention and purpose. They remind us that genius is not about perfection or accolades—it is about progress and contribution.

Embracing the Process of Becoming

One of the most profound lessons of this journey is that genius is not a destination but a process. It is not something we achieve once and for all but something we practice every day. This perspective frees us from the burden of perfection and allows us to focus on growth, learning, and contribution.

As the poet Rainer Maria Rilke wrote, "Be patient toward all that is unsolved in your heart and try to love the questions themselves." The path to genius is filled with questions, challenges, and moments of uncertainty, but it is precisely in these moments that we grow.

For readers, this means embracing the process of becoming with curiosity and courage. It means taking the first step, even when the path is unclear, and trusting that each step will reveal the next. It means celebrating progress, however small, and recognizing that every effort brings you closer to your potential.

The Ripple Effect of Genius

When we unlock our genius, we do more than transform our own lives—we inspire and uplift others. Genius is inherently generative; it creates a ripple effect that extends far beyond ourselves. Our curiosity sparks curiosity in others. Our resilience inspires resilience. Our vision becomes a source of hope and possibility.

Consider the legacy of individuals like Malala Yousafzai, who turned her personal quest for education into a global movement. Her genius lies not only in her courage and determination but in her ability to inspire others to join her cause. Her story reminds us that genius is not about individual glory but about collective impact.

For readers, this ripple effect invites us to consider how our actions and choices influence those around us. By living authentically and pursuing our potential, we create a culture of growth and possibility that benefits not only ourselves but our communities and the world.

A Future of Possibilities

As we conclude this journey, let us look to the future with hope and intention. The principles of genius are not bound by time or circumstance; they are as relevant today as they were in the lives of the great thinkers and leaders who came before us. They offer a blueprint for navigating the complexities of the modern world with clarity, courage, and creativity.

The question is not whether we are capable of

greatness but whether we are willing to pursue it. The world is filled with challenges that call for bold thinking, compassionate leadership, and innovative solutions. The time to answer that call is now.

A Final Charge

To you, the reader: You are capable of genius. You have within you the curiosity to explore, the focus to persevere, the emotional intelligence to connect, the resilience to endure, the vision to dream, and the courage to act. These qualities are not distant ideals—they are seeds waiting to be cultivated.

Take the lessons of this book and make them your own. Let them guide you as you create a life of purpose, growth, and contribution. Remember that greatness is not about what you achieve but about who you become in the process.

The journey ahead will not always be easy, but it will always be worth it. Trust in your ability to navigate the challenges, embrace the opportunities, and unlock the genius within. The world needs your brilliance, your vision, and your courage.

As you close this book, let it mark the beginning of a new chapter—one filled with possibility, progress, and purpose. Go forth and create, inspire, and transform. The call to greatness has been issued. Will you answer it?

ACKNOWLEDGEMENT

This book is the result of countless moments of inspiration, support, and collaboration, and I am deeply grateful to all who made it possible.

To my family and friends, thank you for your unwavering encouragement and belief in my vision. Your support has been the foundation upon which I've built this journey.

To the thinkers, creators, and leaders whose stories illuminate these pages, thank you for your enduring contributions to the world. Your lives have been a wellspring of wisdom and a testament to the boundless potential of the human spirit.

To my editors, designers, and collaborators,

your expertise and dedication have elevated this book in ways I could not have imagined. You are the unsung heroes behind every page.

Finally, to you, the reader—thank you for embarking on this journey. Your curiosity and commitment to growth inspire the very purpose of this book. It is for you that these words were written, and I am honored to share them with you.

With heartfelt gratitude,
Felix Grayson

ABOUT THE AUTHOR

Felix Grayson's journey into timeless wisdom began in childhood, captivated by the stories of philosophers, leaders, and visionaries who shaped the way we think and live. Growing up in a home filled with books, he spent countless hours exploring ideas that asked life's biggest questions—a curiosity that would later define his work.

After facing his own modern challenges—balancing ambition, uncertainty, and the search for meaning—Felix discovered that the wisdom of the past offers profound guidance for the present. This realization became the foundation for the *Stoned Philosopher* series: a collection dedicated to translating ancient insights into practical lessons for today's world.

Felix's writing is more than reflection—it's an invitation to dialogue with history's greatest minds. Through each book, he helps readers find clarity, resilience, and purpose in their own lives—one timeless idea at a time.

When not writing, Felix enjoys quiet contemplation, deep conversation, and exploring the endless pursuit of wisdom in everyday moments.